THE LEGACY CONTINUUM

Building a Multi-Generational Legacy of
Radical Generosity and Kingdom Impact

Richard Leong

Scripture quotations marked (AMPC) are taken from the Amplified® Bible Classic Edition (AMPC), copyright © 1954, 1958, 1962, 1964, 1965, 1987 by The Lockman Foundation. Used by permission. www.Lockman.org.

Scripture quotations marked (ESV) are taken from the ESV® Bible (The Holy Bible, English Standard Version®). ESV® Text Edition: 2016. Copyright © 2001 by Crossway, a publishing ministry of Good News Publishers. The ESV® text has been reproduced in cooperation with and by permission of Good News Publishers. Unauthorized reproduction of this publication is prohibited. Used by permission. All rights reserved.

Scripture quotations marked (ISV) are taken from the Holy Bible: International Standard Version®. Copyright © 1995–2014 by The ISV Foundation. All rights reserved internationally. Used by permission of Davidson Press, LLC.

Scripture quotations marked (KJV) are taken from the King James Bible. Accessed on Bible Gateway. www.BibleGateway.com.

Scripture marked (MSG) are taken from The Message, copyright © 1993, 2002, 2018 by Eugene H. Peterson. Used by permission of NavPress. All rights reserved. Represented by Tyndale House Publishers, Inc.

Scripture quotations marked (NET) are taken from the NET Bible® copyright © 1996–2017 by Biblical Studies Press, L.L.C. http://netbible.com All rights reserved.

Scripture quotations marked (NIV) are taken from the Holy Bible, New International Version®, NIV® Copyright © 1973, 1978, 1984, 2011 by Biblica, Inc.® Used by permission. All rights reserved worldwide.

Scripture quotations marked (NLT) are taken from the Holy Bible, New Living Translation (NLT), copyright © 1996, 2004, 2015 by Tyndale House Foundation. Used by permission of Tyndale House Publishers, Inc., Carol Stream, Illinois 60188. All rights reserved.

Renown Publishing
www.renownpublishing.com

The Legacy Continuum / Richard Leong
ISBN-13: 978-1-952602-89-4

Praise for *The Legacy Continuum*

Inevitably, we all ask the question, "What am I doing with my life?" With inspiring stories and practical modeling, *Legacy Continuum* will persuade you to take hold of the life-changing impact we all can make in our relationships and the world around us, compelled by a spirit of generosity and hope. In these challenging days, we need this book more than ever!

David Kim, CEO, Co-Founder of Goldenwood

Richard's book is a rich trove of biblical truth, practical nuggets for our journey, and wisdom gained from looking back and carrying it forward. This "handbook" will be one I refer back to as I continue asking its soul-probing questions—in hopes of creating a legacy that brings glory to the King.

Heather Tuininga, Principal of 10|10 Strategies

This book is full of wisdom and kindness. Richard is a fatherly guide who can help you identify and successfully pass along your family's true assets and bring blessing to the world. Whether you are thinking about these issues for the first time or have a plan in place, you will benefit from his probing questions and practical ideas.

Eric Fleshood, CEO of Cru Foundation

An inheritance is not simply a gift. In the original meaning, it was also an assignment and a responsibility for the next generation. I love the way Richard Leong reminds us of the generations of stories, values, dreams, and character we have to draw on as part of our own story. That story is a chapter in a larger book that is added to by our children and theirs. It may take hundreds of years and a stream of generations to accomplish the work of God. Our life is connected to those who came before and those who follow. Our lives are chapters in a novel whose author has woven us together to accomplish His purpose—one life at a time.

Fred Smith, Founder of The Gathering

Everyone should read this book! Richard has done an amazing job of sharing stories while making a case for why we all should focus on creating a lasting legacy not just as individuals, but also as families and communities. Legacy, purpose, mission, generosity, and responsibility, all themes in this book, result in our ability to have an intentional, positive impact for the Kingdom. True joy and fulfillment comes from walking in our calling, where we will make the most difference. Not only does Richard encourage us to embrace this mindset and lifestyle, but he also outlines step by step how to achieve it.

Dr. Ken Keis, Award Winning Author of *The Quest For Purpose* and *Why Aren't You More Like Me?*

This book has the potential to change your legacy and the future legacy of your family. It is intentional, inspirational, and inspired by God. Richard has created a blueprint for succession planning. A must-read!

Terry Smith, Retired President of Smith Gardens

This book, *The Legacy Continuum*, reads as though Jesus is whispering in your ear and saying, "It's not money, but rather relationships within the family that determine how long your legacy will last." Then, Leong shares the words Jesus gives to all of us, multiple times throughout the Bible, to help keep us on track. His own story is a revelation of how he began to listen, and his and his family's lives changed forever! Understanding where your gifts come from, and how you can prepare your family to nurture them boldly so that every generation can enjoy one another, requires they hold the family baton in a way that inspires future generations to feel connected! And Richard reveals how *process* will get you there.

Jerry Nuerge, Founder of Family Meridian (an Organization Helping Families Flourish for Multiple Generations) and Author of Multiple Books

Managing money, teaching our children, and leaving a legacy are all things commanded in Scripture. Jesus spoke a lot about money, but how do we leave a legacy that extends beyond our lifetime, and our children's and grandchildren's lifetimes? Richard Leong gives us this map to guide us through stewarding the resources God has blessed us with. Through solid wisdom, practical life stories, scriptural references, and clear, sound advice, Richard Leong gives us the answer.

Michael Chung, Ph.D., Pastor at Wheaton Chinese Alliance Church | Author of *Leadership Is Destiny: 52 Lessons from the Life of David*

We all long to impact generations beyond us. Yet, we often find those conversations perplexing or intimidating in real life! From a practical standpoint, and I mean really "brass tacks," how do we gracefully pass the baton multi-generationally in our families as followers of Christ? Good news: Richard decodes much of it. I feel grateful for his open conversations about what worked, what didn't, and how God in His perfectness meets Richard's family in both scenarios as they journey together! As you endeavor to create your lasting family legacy, you might seek courage; maybe a framework for engaging with your family, or tips and ideas; perhaps restored energy after past failed attempts. Wherever your family story sits today, Richard has something special for you.

Joe Eelkema, Gift Advisor for National Christian Foundation California

"Clarify your purpose." "Fight the good fight." "Live for something greater than yourself." We've all heard messages like these. In *The Legacy Continuum*, Richard inspires us through his journey and gives us an incredibly practical framework for applying these principles to our lives here and now. This book will guide, encourage, challenge, and inspire you to take the practical steps necessary to live life with laser focus and "redeem the time" entrusted to you. If you want a guide to help you make a generational impact and Kingdom difference in your world, Richard Leong is your man, and this book is your roadmap.

Rob Rogers, Senior Pastor of Grace Chapel

Richard's advice is crystal clear, and a must-read for anyone who wants to leave a lasting and positive legacy on this earth.

Sybil Ackerman-Munson, President of Ackerman-Munson Strategies and Do Your Good LLC

Richard has written a book that all Christian families need to read through. The simple lessons, illustrations, and on-point information have me thinking about our family legacy from a whole new perspective. The framework is easy to apply, and Richard shares tips, suggestions, and questions to help you get started. After reading this book, I've thought of several others I need to share it with. Like me, after reading this book, you won't look at how you use your time, talent, and treasure in the same way again.

Kyle Gillette, CCO of SAGE Mindset Coaching | Author of
SAGE Leadership - A 4-Part Framework to Becoming a People First Leader

I highly recommend *The Legacy Continuum!* Having known Richard Leong for over fifteen years and walked with him through many of the conversations highlighted in these pages, I can attest to the fact that he genuinely lives out the timely principles he writes about in this remarkable read. *The Legacy Continuum* is an excellent and inspirational book with practical guidelines on how to think through and implement strategies that are sure to leave a positive impact on our world today. Embracing these truths will do much to strengthen our families and enable us all to leave a legacy that I believe is God-ordained!

Paul B. Thompson, President and Chief Investment Officer of Ascension Capital Advisors, Inc.

All Christ followers want to lead a life that brings glory and honor to God. Many also want the next generation(s) to follow in their footsteps, yet they feel clueless as to how to bring this desire to fruition. In this very personal recounting of a family's journey, Rich Leong lays out for us the roadmap for a legacy continuum that would transform not only future generations but also those involved in enriching and preserving [this legacy]. The fact that Rich is so gracious in sharing his and his family's tireless labor to press toward such a goal of high calling (Philippians 3:13–14) is itself a testament to the generosity that must underpin the legacy of every Christian who is serious about their purpose-driven life.

Ernest Liang, Ph.D., Director of Center for Christianity in Business | Associate Professor of Finance | Editor of *Christian Business Review,* Archie W. Dunham College of Business, Houston Baptist University

Leaving a legacy is not for the faint of heart. It involves more than just leaving your imprint on the face of a building or a business. It involves time, purpose, and intentionality of imprinting your God-honoring values upon the life of your family and those you serve in Jesus' name. Richard shares his legacy journey with such vulnerability and clarity that you will feel inspired to examine the character and focus of your life's legacy. Enjoy the journey.

Steve Perry, author of *Living With Wealth Without Losing Your Soul* and *The Accidental Philanthropist*

To my heavenly Father, who gave me a legacy worth living and passing on.

...so the next generation would know, and all the generations to come—know the truth and tell the stories so their children can trust in God...

—Psalm 78:6 (MSG)

CONTENTS

Foreword by
Kendra VanderMeulen

Over the last fifteen years, as the President of National Christian Northwest and now the CEO of NCF, I have had the privilege of walking alongside many families as they seek to be great stewards of all that God has entrusted to them. As part of this work, our team has poured ourselves into building a community of generous givers who are committed to walking together to grow in generosity and to spread the message to more and more people. It was in this context that I met Richard and Elina Leong. They were longtime NCF givers, but when they attended a Journey of Generosity retreat, they immediately grasped the significance of the message and joined us by investing themselves in the community of generous givers.

In our narcissistic culture, which values self-realization over everything else, it is a challenge to put God's truths around money and legacy first. The Lord makes it clear that all we are and all we have are His. He gave us everything for our joy and His glory, and we are to manage it for His purposes, which include caring for our families, our communities, and the world and completing the Great Commission. These goals are much bigger than our little lives, but we have a part in them, and finishing the race well is what this book addresses.

Over these years, I have enjoyed the gift of knowing and serving Richard and Elina Leong in their journey. We have spent many hours talking about the best ways to steward the wealth entrusted to them and have also worked to open opportunities for more and more people in our region to experience the life-changing message of biblical generosity. They have been faithful stewards of much and, more than most couples, have worked hard to prepare the next generation to understand the legacy that started before Richard and Elina and extends through them to their daughters and grandchildren. Their deepest desire is that this legacy will be one of world-changing biblical generosity.

For most people, living a life of generosity here and now, day to day, is a big enough challenge. Richard and Elina took the further bold step to consider what has come before them and to reflect on the way those relationships formed them, for better or worse. They then spent time sorting out what to treasure and carry forward from that past and what to embrace from their own life experiences to produce a story of generosity to share with the next generation. However, they did not stop with handing this story to their daughters. They humbly invited their daughters' stories into their story to expand the Legacy Continuum beyond themselves and into the future.

In this book, you will hear and see that legacy is not just about you. It is about those who came before you and those who will come after you. Developing a lasting legacy of biblical generosity involves being intentional, humble, patient, and determined. You must fight for the future of your family by loving them, engaging them, and developing a vision for the future together. You will need to be aware of the enemy and his desire to derail you by discouraging you. You will need to work to equip your family to run this race for the long term so they can pass the baton to the next generation and so on, for generations to come. Richard and Elina share their story and the lessons they have learned generously and transparently.

I love their mission statement: "Two Tunics Legacy is an expression of God's abounding generosity. Our mission is to live out and promote the call to action in Luke 3:11. We do this by engaging, challenging, and partnering with others to visibly demonstrate the power of God's provision and compassion to a world in need." This mission statement is God-centered and so reflective of who God has made Richard and Elina to be, and it does not stop there. They developed the mission statement with their two daughters, Vivian and Vanessa, such that it reflects their style of generosity as well. I hope that I have the privilege of seeing how it plays out through them and through their children as well.

I know from personal experience how challenging it can be to manage this topic of legacy with purpose and faith.

Families are busy. Relationships are complicated. Each person has his or her own perspective on all matters, including the meaning of money and the questions around its biblical uses. This book is a gift from a person who has taken this journey more seriously than most and who has stepped back from the process to extract key lessons to share, first with his own family and now with us. I am grateful for the effort Richard has put in and for his generosity in sharing the lessons he has learned with us. I think you will be grateful as well.

If you are hoping to finish your race well and you are asking questions about how to do it God's way, you will want to examine Scripture first and then read the stories of others who have walked this path before you. This is one of those stories, and it is well worth the read. I pray that the Lord uses this book to inspire and encourage you along the way.

Kendra VanderMeulen
CEO, National Christian Foundation

A Lasting Legacy

What do you want to accomplish before you die?

I'm not talking about crossing items off your bucket list, though climbing Mount Everest sounds like a great goal. I'm talking about day-to-day life. I'm talking about how you choose to spend your time and the causes that get the most of your attention.

I'm talking about life purpose—and not just any life purpose. I'm talking about the kind of life purpose that leads to a lasting legacy that can begin now, not later.

Experts tell us that millennials care about doing meaningful work.[1][2] They're not so much driven by dollars as they are by purpose. They enjoy being part of a team and collaborating. They also value their freedom of choice; autonomy is key for them. With that kind of profile, you would think that the last thing millennials would want is to drift haphazardly through life, yet the yearning for purpose and meaning and the exercise of autonomy and choice can all too easily result in aimlessness. Millennials may find themselves chasing the next big possibility that seems to hold the promise of greater fulfillment, whether it be a trip around the world or a job change. But when the excitement fades, they are back where they started, longing for more meaning and purpose.

Meanwhile, baby boomers spent decades building their pensions. While millennials understand the importance of doing meaningful work now, boomers understand the importance of having something to pass along. Both views are good. However, as the saying goes, too much of a good thing is never good enough. Balance, in my opinion, is needed.

You see, legacy isn't just a topic for older people, nor is it a topic solely tied to death and dying. There is no rule that your legacy can start only after you've passed. No matter how old you are, no matter your net worth or beliefs on the topic, you are building a legacy right now. The decisions you make and the life you live are building your legacy.

Whether we realize it or not, we're building a legacy that will get passed on to future generations, but I believe that we have a calling and a responsibility to be intentional about legacy. That said, legacy is more than curating an Instagram profile of once-in-a-lifetime experiences, and it's certainly more than a life of striving or a fuzzy feeling you get while on an emotional high. So, the question is: What kind of legacy are you building? Are you intentional about how your life impacts those around you and those who will come after you? Do you see the bigger picture? Do you realize that you have a role to play in a much bigger game?

MY JOURNEY FROM CORPORATE LADDER
TO LEAVING A LASTING LEGACY

God has blessed me with a full and rewarding life, but it certainly hasn't been easy. I grew up in one of the most notorious public housing projects in Brooklyn, New York. I encountered the ugliness of discrimination at a very young age, and I faced academic challenges and setbacks that threatened my future. By sheer determination, a strong work ethic, divine intervention, and the help of very loving people, I earned an engineering degree and worked my way into the executive ranks of corporate America.

For decades, I climbed the corporate ladder and traveled the world, thinking that I had reached the pinnacle of my life calling. While I might have been living the American dream, I realized over time that my legacy was nominal. Sure, I had money to pass on to my children, but was that all I had to offer them? What about the lessons learned, the wisdom gained, my fluctuating faith journey, and the view of life that had shaped me? Would those things become lost once I passed away? Most importantly, did God intend for my cumulative life's work to be nothing more than a shoebox of photos and a last will and testament?

In the first edition of Webster's dictionary, in 1828, *wealth* is defined as: "1. Prosperity; external happiness. 2. Riches; large possessions of money, goods or land; that abundance of worldly estate which exceeds estate of the greater part of the community; affluence; opulence."[3] And

3

prosperity is defined as: "Advance or gain in any thing good or desirable."[4] One writer posits that by taking both of these definitions into consideration, we can determine that wealth means "an advance or gain in anything good or desirable toward the health and benefit of others."[5]

In other words, wealth is not solely monetary. It's not only your net worth and investment portfolio. Wealth also isn't your collection of personal experiences. True wealth transcends money, riches, and stamps in your passport. *True wealth benefits others.*

When I first started thinking about legacy, it was mind-blowing to realize that what I do during my life could have an influence on people living decades from now. By pouring into the lives of others, I have the opportunity to change their future. By passing on the things I've learned and the family stories that have shaped me, I can better prepare my children and grandchildren, and they can, in turn, prepare future generations.

Beyond that, my faith compels me to leave an inheritance to the generations after me. Proverbs 13:22 reads, "A good man leaves an inheritance to his children's children, but the sinner's wealth is laid up for the righteous" (ESV). This inheritance entails not just money, but also generosity and Kingdom impact.

I also realized that when my family comes on board and joins me in these efforts, when we become a team running the race of life together, then the things we do, the faith we hold dear, the money we give, and the wisdom we pass down multiply.

This shift in my mindset was substantial and immediately produced a ripple effect that will impact generations to come. From that point on, I became focused on legacy—true legacy.

WE ARE NOT MEANT TO RUN ALONE

It took a while to get my team ready for the race. Don't get me wrong; it wasn't because my family wasn't receptive to the idea. When my wife and I organized our first meeting to discuss our family legacy, our daughters' faces showed their eagerness to learn about our family history and how we could use the past to inform the present and change the future. But it has been a process. We've spent years figuring out how to run this race together, and we've experienced a lot of bumps along the way. Even with all of the setbacks, something beautiful has come out of our faithfulness.

My family meets regularly and with intentionality. We ask such questions as:

- How can we impact the world around us?

- How can our faith inform our generosity toward others and how we choose to give?

- How can we speak into the lives of those who will follow us?

These are the kinds of questions we deal with, and it's been incredible to see the change that has come as a result of these discussions.

1. We are more Kingdom-minded. We believe that God wants us to live intentionally and to grow and expand His Kingdom through our generosity.

2. We are more effective. We've found that when we approach legacy as a group, our money, our ideas, and our efforts go much further.

3. We are more united. Going into this, I thought that I had a good relationship with my wife and daughters, but God has brought Elina, Vivian, Vanessa, and me even closer. I am continually astounded by how much more unified we are now, especially in our resolve to make a difference in the world for God. We are more united because we now share a common family legacy and a vision to extend that legacy for many generations.

While this process has been a journey and didn't happen overnight (much to my dismay!), the results have been worth every painful discussion, every disagreement, every setback, every detour along the way. The incredible blessings that we see as a result of our unity and intentionality are like plants that we've cultivated and nurtured over time. Now we are experiencing the joy of generosity. We are yielding a plentiful harvest and then turning around and planting new seeds.

And here's the best part: what we've been able to do, the change that has happened in our lives as a result of our shift in focus toward lasting legacy, is available to you and your family, too.

It Starts Now

I was never particularly good at high school track. I wasn't the fastest or the strongest. I didn't have the most endurance or the best natural ability. What I did have was a desire to be part of the team, to do my best, to learn and grow, and to contribute what I could to the overall cause.

Over time, my coach was able to shape me. He helped me to improve my time, my stride, and my endurance. On my own, I was never a star, but when I was part of my team, when I was part of something much bigger than myself, my contribution was needed. That's when I saw my hard work pay off.

When the Apostle Paul saw himself nearing the end of his Christian journey on earth, the Christian race, he wrote, "I have fought the good fight, I have finished the race, I have kept the faith. Henceforth there is laid up for me the crown of righteousness, which the Lord, the righteous judge, will award to me on that day, and not only to me but also to all who have loved his appearing" (2 Timothy 4:7–8 ESV). Notice how Paul didn't write about personal accomplishment or prowess. He wrote about faithfulness during the race and the reward that comes to everyone who sticks it out all the way to the finish line.

In this book, I'm going to reveal to you the power of your legacy. More importantly, we're going to talk about how your family can work together as a team, each using his or her strengths and gifts, to impact future generations and multiply your efforts.

It's not about padding your bank account or even filling your life with good works. It's about being intentional in your generosity, legacy, and Kingdom impact through faithfully training, growing, and then doing.

Whether you wish it or not, your legacy will be passed on to future generations. You will leave behind a life, good or bad, that will impact others. The beauty is that your legacy is still being written. The race is still being run, and you are invited to join the track team regardless of your current running skills.

In this busy world that we live in, it's not easy to find the time to be intentional and to talk with family about legacy. While it may not be *easy* or *convenient*, it is *possible*, and God is calling you to begin this journey.

You have the power to speak into the lives of your descendants. You have the ability to *do good* in the here and now. Yes, you are flawed. No, you may not always feel like a leader, but God has a place for you and a plan for your life and your family line. It's time to find out what that is.

PART ONE:
ON YOUR MARK

CHAPTER ONE

Preparing Your Legacy

A good man leaves an inheritance to his children's children....

—Proverbs 13:22a (ESV)

In the context of a track meet, the *mark* is the starting point for a foot race. When given the command "on your mark," runners move to their respective places on the track, knowing that the race is about to begin.

When they take their marks, they are prepared. They've put in the hard work. They understand the race, and they know their role in it.

If we think about life as a race, then it's important to make sure that we are ready to run it. It's important that when we take our marks, we do so confidently. Unlike a competitive race, a Christian's race lasts a lifetime, and it's not always the fastest or strongest who wins.

Preparing for your race starts with developing a clear vision for why God placed you here on earth and what impact

He wants you to have. In this chapter, I will share God-sized concepts that have fueled my passion to create and implement my legacy plan, and I hope that these concepts will inspire you to do the same. The future of your family is at stake!

MY STORY

I'm living the American Dream. Despite growing up in poverty, my work ethic, faith, and perseverance pushed me to succeed in life. I graduated college with an engineering degree, which allowed me to work for several elite global companies in the energy field. I climbed the corporate ladder and reached the executive ranks. I've made my fair share of mistakes, but I could also fill pages and pages with my successes and accomplishments, with my wife, who has stood by me for forty-eight years, and my family, who have brought me immeasurable joy.

All of this wouldn't have been possible without the legacy that my parents and grandparents left me. Now I will leave a legacy, built upon what they gave me, to my children, my grandchildren, and the world. When you leave a quality legacy, it impacts generation after generation.

Let me start at the beginning.

China was a land ravaged by war and economic strife, so my dad's family made immeasurable sacrifices to send him to America. They knew that if they invested in him and his future, it could change the entire family for generations to come.

My dad came to the U. S. and worked hard, but it wasn't easy. He was Chinese and had limited English-speaking skills. His job prospects were dismal. He worked as a waiter, relying on tips as his major source of income, so it was difficult for him to support a wife and three kids. What little extra he had went to our family back in China to help bring them out of terrible poverty. Meanwhile, we lived in a converted storeroom near Chinatown, Manhattan. We had one window, at least, but we had no proper heating (the stove doubled as our heat source), and I remember my dad paying off a $20 icebox in monthly installments. That was how tight our finances were.

By the 1950s, we were living just above the poverty level, which qualified us to move into newly built public housing: the Farragut housing project in Brooklyn, New York. It felt like the most incredible upgrade. We'd never had such luxury.

But over time, the neighborhood shifted. We encountered the ugliness of discrimination, bullying, and violence, and it was all I could do to keep my head down and struggle my way through school.

This was the beginning that shaped me. Extreme poverty in China led to my uneducated parents doing what they could to make it in a foreign country with modest means. Their goal? To change the family's future. There was little in their bank account, yet they gifted me something much more valuable than an inheritance or a trust fund. They gifted me a philosophy of life, one passed down to them from their parents.

This philosophy consists of a strong work ethic, a pride in heritage and culture, a disciplined life, a focus on family, and the courage to press on and not back down. They showed me how the brave actions of one generation can impact generations to come. Their legacy set me up for success, and it's what fuels my own legacy.

Your legacy is not just about you. In fact, all our lives are affected by the legacies of those who have gone before us, and in turn, our lives affect those who come after us.

HAVE YOU THOUGHT ABOUT YOUR LEGACY?

I once came across an online chat room where the topic was legacy. One gentleman shared, "I don't care about legacy aside from being a good person who does good things. Sure, I might try to accomplish certain things in life and business, but I do these things for myself and my kids. I'm not going to fool myself into thinking that I can leave a real legacy."

I encounter people with this mindset all the time, and it saddens me. This approach devalues contributions to family and future. It disregards the stories of the past, stories of ancestors who fought and sacrificed for a better way. It assumes that what we do today will not matter a hundred years from now. These same people who deny their potential to leave a legacy are searching for the meaning of life. They strive to find purpose yet disregard the role that legacy plays in purpose and meaning.

I also come across people who tend to think about their legacy in terms of an estate. They plan to let an attorney handle it, even the division of assets. Some of them fear retaliation if one heir is treated differently from another. Others are glad that they have the papers written up and filed away. They'd prefer never to deal with it again! Each of these approaches treats legacy as if it's a bother, a necessary evil.

Others treat legacy as if it's a burden. *"What do I do with all this stuff?"* I come across this question all the time, most recently from an eighty-year-old whose estate has a large pot of money. People with this mindset tend to have the right investments and a lifetime's worth of possessions, but as they near the end of their lives, they don't know what to do with all that they've accumulated.

Of course, they've been told to leave it to their descendants, but as time goes on, they begin to question if amassing money and material possessions in this way was the right thing to do. They begin to wonder how many people they could have helped over the years if they'd been more giving. They begin to wonder what kind of an impact they could have had if they'd been more focused on others instead of themselves and their families. They wonder how much more meaningful their lives could have been if they'd been a bit less stringent in their retirement plans.

I don't blame them. Our natural inclination is to leave everything to our heirs, but the real question is whether that's the right thing to do and if it will yield the best results in the long run.

The greatest transference of wealth in history is now taking place: "Baby Boomers, the generation of people born between 1944 and 1964, are expected to transfer $30 trillion in wealth to younger generations over the next many years. This jaw-dropping amount has led many journalists and financial experts to refer to the gradual event as the 'great wealth transfer.'"[6] Sadly, studies show that 70 percent of families lose their stored-up wealth by the second generation.[7]

Think of what that money could do. Think about the Kingdom good that could happen if people were to take even a fraction of that and push it out into the world to restore and renew it.

This is what happens when people invest too much time amassing wealth and their entire legacy is wrapped up in a last will and testament. This is what happens when we focus too much on the finish line and not enough on giving our resources today in ways that will impact the future. Keep in mind that our resources are more than just our money; they include our time and talent as well.

So, I ask you: Have you thought about your legacy? If you have, are you living your legacy now?

Are you living in the moment, doing good to those around you? Or are you looking out for you and yours, solely focused on storing up a treasure that may seem less meaningful once you're in your final years? I am reminded of Matthew 6:19–21, which reads, "Do not lay up for yourselves treasures on earth, where moth and rust destroy and where thieves break in and steal, but lay up for yourselves treasures in heaven, where neither moth nor rust destroys and where thieves do not break in and steal. For where your treasure is, there your heart will be also" (ESV).

LEGACY AND THE MEANING OF LIFE
ACCORDING TO THE BIBLE

The Bible tells us that everything on earth belongs to the Lord (Psalm 24:1). James 1:17 expands on this, saying that all gifts come from God. His generosity is proven in the gift of His Son, Jesus (Romans 8:31–32). Since the world is God's and everything good comes from Him, we can know that meaning and purpose come from God. But what does God want us to do with the good things He gives us?

In Proverbs 27:23–24, Solomon advised his shepherds, "Be sure you know the condition of your flocks, give careful attention to your herds; for riches do not endure forever, and a crown is not secure for all generations" (NIV). From this we know that we are to be good stewards, because the good things we have today may not be there for future generations if we are not careful. So yes, we are to save and invest, but we can't stop there. The next step is to be conscientious and to look after the well-being of others.

Scripture also tells us, "One person gives freely, yet gains even more; another withholds unduly, but comes to poverty. A generous person will prosper; whoever refreshes others will be refreshed. People curse the one who hoards grain, but they pray God's blessing on the one who is willing to sell" (Proverbs 11:24–26 NIV). From this we know that generosity is the goal. God gives to us so that we can steward what He gives us and then bless others with it.

Furthermore, 1 Timothy 6:17 teaches that we should not

trust in money. We should trust in God, who gives us all we need for living fully. This means that generosity and goodness do not necessarily have a dollar sign! Being generous with our time and talent can be even more impactful than writing a check.

If all good things come from God, including our meaning and purpose, and we are to be good stewards and be generous, then what is the end game? What is the ultimate goal?

We are to be focused on living a life of meaning, a *living legacy* for future generations. When God blessed Abraham, the blessing wasn't just for Abraham and his children. It was for all of Abraham's descendants and, even more importantly, for all of the earth.

When Moses was ready to die, he explained the vision God had given him. He talked about what he wanted for his people. He talked about God's blessing on the entire nation of Israel for generations to come.

God's goodness starts with us, and then it pours out onto others. The life meaning He gives starts with us and pours out onto others. And that life meaning quickly becomes a legacy that starts now and pours out onto the rest of the world.

CREATING A LIFE OF MEANING

Understanding who you are in Christ and living out your faith in the way He intends is the first step to creating a life of meaning and a legacy. Of course, this is easy to say and hard to do.

God's call is clear that we are to live in obedience to Him

and in kindness and generosity toward others as we work toward the renewal and restoration of a lost world. However, we tend to get lost in the day-to-day.

For too many years, my mission was my vocation. It became my idol, the thing that I clung to with everything I had. I assumed that since I was successful in it, my career represented my life's meaning. I assumed that it was my legacy. I justified this by telling myself that it was my vocation that provided a good life for my family, so it was good and right for me to put all of my energy toward it. But really, my vocation was just stroking my ego. As I climbed the ladder, my career became my obsession.

Then, in my fifties, I began to think about legacy. At first, I equated my legacy to "stuff" and how my investments and possessions would be dispersed after I died. But over time, God put wonderful people in my life who mentored me and encouraged me toward my personal mission: to use generosity to fuel a life of meaning.

Generosity is more than an action. It is a state of being, an attitude, a way of life. The more I dug in, the more I found that God had already been planting in me seeds of generosity for quite some time. In my working years, I invested in those around me and helped others to climb the corporate ladder. I was generous with my time and talent, and once I realized that generosity had always been part of who I was, everything flowed from there.

Generosity has become part of my identity. It's who I am, who I've always wanted to be. Pursuing generosity has helped me to find meaning in my life and to build a legacy.

Generosity is my key, and I believe that it's your key, too, but here's what's really neat: the way you best live out generosity will look very different from the way I live out generosity. To uncover how generosity fits into your life, it's important to ask yourself some tough questions:

- What passions has God given you to change the world?

- What do you suppose breaks God's heart in the world today? What will you do about it?

- What dreams or desires do you have to help restore and renew a lost world?

The answers to these questions are not wishful thinking! They come from God, and here's where it gets interesting. When we step into our God-given identity, we begin to develop a meaningful legacy in the here and now. It's then that generosity will flow.

WHAT IS THE LEGACY CONTINUUM?

We're not talking about a legacy that exists for a short time once you die. We're talking about a living legacy that draws upon the legacy of your ancestors and now flows through you, impacting everyone around you today and for generations to come. I call it the *Legacy Continuum*.

The Legacy Continuum is my term for describing the potential Kingdom impact you and your family could have on the world by looking at a multi-generational approach to generosity. It leverages the efforts of those before us and shows the unbounded potential of future generations. To help you visualize what I'm talking about, I put together this graphic:

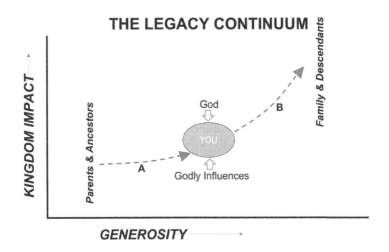

This graphic shows the impact of your life and the lives of your ancestors and descendants. By drawing from the past, building on the present, and pouring yourself into future generations, you have it within your power to grow the collective Kingdom impact on the world through increasing generosity at an exponential rate.

God's way of impacting the world is by making human beings instruments of change when they truly follow His Son, Jesus Christ. This is what the Lord Jesus meant when He called His disciples "the salt of the earth" and "the light of the world" (Matthew 5:13–14 NIV) and when He said, "...apart from me you can do nothing" (John 15:5 NIV). This is the essence of real Kingdom impact.

To further understand Kingdom impact, consider this definition:[8]

> Kingdom Impact is really about the marrying of resources with God-sized results. This means that Kingdom Impact is not something that people can do—it is something that God must do. But God chose to work through us in this world so we have an opportunity to share in that impact.

You can use this graphic to see how you've met various needs, such as poverty, homelessness, and caring for widows and orphans. You can also use it to check how you and others have made use of your time, talent, and treasure and how you've built up the body of Christ spiritually, physically, and mentally. This graphic will help you to discern the level of impact you've had on the world around you.

The line that I've charted represents an ideal scenario, showing how the more generous we are, the greater Kingdom impact we will have. It also shows how this impact builds on itself if we pursue Kingdom generosity generation after generation.

Line A includes everything we received from those before us, including our beliefs, values, faith, and possessions. This should fuel or, at the very least, inform your legacy. **Line B** represents your contribution to your generational legacy. It's your vision for a family legacy, and it shows what can happen should your descendants continue with the vision and expand on it for generations to come.

And right there in the middle is where **you** are. You are front and center in this process. You determine how your family's past legacy will look going forward. Every family's Legacy Continuum will look different. While the graph here displays an ideal curve, most families' legacies are a lot messier than this, and that's okay. Perhaps your parents and grandparents were much more Kingdom-minded than you currently are. Or perhaps there was a dip in your Continuum when your family didn't live as generously for a period of time.

It doesn't matter what your A line looks like. All that matters is what you choose to do today and the impact you have on that B line. The way you steepen Line B is by increasing your generosity toward Kingdom efforts. The really great part of this is how a relatively small change in one factor can have an outsized impact on another factor. This is what I call the *multiplier effect*. By drawing from the past, building on the present, and pouring yourself into future generations, you can steepen the Continuum and produce a multiplier effect, by which a relatively small amount of increase in family generosity results in a greater Kingdom impact.

As you bring the rest of your family into this mindset of legacy living, handing the baton to them in the relay race of life, you'll soon find that the impact of your collective generosity grows faster and greater than the impact you could have on your own.

IMPACT FUTURE GENERATIONS

You'd be amazed how my family's conversations have shifted since we started focusing on generosity. Instead of talking about our favorite restaurants and television shows, we talk about ways to help others and needs that we see around us and in the world.

One of my daughters, Vivian, and my son-in-law, Jason, are now raising their children to live with legacy in mind. They're going through Dave Ramsey's Financial Peace University (the version for kids) and are laying a foundation of stewardship and generosity. Their family conversations are deeper and more Kingdom-centric, and my eldest grandson is working through these concepts while he is in middle school!

Impacting and investing in future generations is possible, and we can choose to begin today. Doing so will build character and yield spirituality and financial confidence.

This might look like setting up small trust funds for college or continuing education. It might look like creating family traditions, such as an annual gathering to discuss your giving goals and enhance relationships. It might look like taking part in generous endeavors together. My family has put together a legacy fund that we use to impact others. This fund is the baton that will last for multiple generations, and it's something that we actively maintain and build together.

We'll go into some of these possibilities in greater depth in upcoming chapters, but I want to plant the seed now. It's possible to give future generations a family identity that they can be proud of, one that will feed their confidence and self-awareness and empower them to be changemakers in their own lives.

HOW TO LIVE OUT YOUR LEGACY

The process of planning and implementing your legacy will provide you with a road map for how to live today. It will bring into full view what your purpose in life is, how you should be living, and how you should manage the three critical aspects of your life: your time, talent, and treasure.

If you are a person of faith, spending the time early on to assess where you are with God could make the difference between living a Spirit-filled life of hope and confidence and being driven by fear and worry. Once this road map is complete (with tweaks along the way), it then becomes a compass to ensure that you are living out your life as planned.

Thinking in terms of your legacy will bring into full view the things that should be the most important in your life, such as your faith, family, friends, church, and community. Although legacy planning is more about the here and now, it will also inform your estate planning as you work to ensure that your living legacy will continue after you are gone.

As you assess your life and make changes, it's also important to find accountability outside of your family members. This should be a group of like-minded people who can encourage you, help you, and expand what you think is possible. While they are helping you to shape your Legacy Continuum, you can help them to shape theirs as well.

The more you step into your meaningful legacy, the more

you will see ways you can offer your time, talent, or treasure, and sometimes you may find that you can offer all three! The times when I've seen the greatest impact are when I've paired my monetary donations with active involvement and use of my talent. It's a simple formula that benefits both you and the recipient in incredible ways:

$$\text{Involvement} \times \text{Insight} \times \text{Money} = \text{Kingdom Impact}$$

Giving money blindly may yield some impact, but giving money alongside your involvement and deeper insight into the organization will yield an even larger impact. This is wisdom that I've picked up along the way, leading to an even bigger and better generosity boost than I ever thought possible!

TIME FOR THE RACE OF YOUR LIFE

In a sermon, the Reverend Canon Philip R. Taylor said, "We are indeed running, always running, in a world of runners and seekers, after what we think are God's promises. We live in a world where many see and believe in a God who promises fame, fortune, health, peace, prosperity, power, and temporal salvation, and so we run after these promises."[9]

While we may think that the best thing is to run after the riches of the world, the Bible tells us that the race worth running is the race for faith. Paul wrote in 2 Timothy 4:7, "I have fought the good fight, I have finished the race, I have kept the faith" (ESV).

It's important to remember, however, that the best runners are ones who are fully prepared. Paul "Bear" Bryant, the head coach of the University of Alabama, said it best: "It's not the will to win that matters—everyone has that. It's the will to prepare to win that matters." [10] I want this to sink in. You can't run a race if you haven't even trained for it. When my family and I first moved to Bellingham in 2014, I decided that it was time for me to practice radical generosity. This kind of generosity isn't about how you give; it's about the way you live. The way I pursued radical generosity was to look for local causes that I could support beyond our usual involvement with the church.

I was soon introduced to the executive director of the local rescue mission. He had recently assumed this position, and after a few conversations with him, it became apparent that he needed help to think more strategically about how he would move the ninety-year-old organization forward. This was a perfect fit for my background in corporate strategy planning, so I poured everything I had into helping him to shape the mission. We met steadily for over a year and developed a solid mentoring relationship that went both ways. I learned so much about homelessness, and he learned about the importance of strategic thinking as a leader of a nonprofit.

I wasn't writing him big checks at that time. I wasn't looking to have a new building dedicated in my name. I was giving him what I believed he needed most, which just happened to be something I'd been training in and perfecting for decades.

This is the sort of generosity that leaves a legacy, and that's what I want for you. As you go to your mark before the race begins, take time to consider how your life might exemplify generosity. If you were to focus on and pursue generosity, how might your relationships change? How might your finances change? How might you spend your time differently? Would you see the end of your life in a more enlightened way?

These are the questions that will set you up for success as you train to run the race.

Chapter One Notes

CHAPTER TWO

Assessing the True Value of Your Asset Portfolio

Do not lay up for yourselves treasures on earth, where moth and rust destroy and where thieves break in and steal, but lay up for yourselves treasures in heaven, where neither moth nor rust destroys and where thieves do not break in and steal. For where your treasure is, there your heart will be also.

—Matthew 6:19–21 *(ESV)*

In Chapter One, we talked about why legacy matters. Knowing about legacy and understanding how your legacy can impact future generations is crucial to running the Christian race. Before you can take your mark and begin the race, you need to understand how your legacy is unique. In other words, how does your story inform the type of legacy that you will leave? Or, to continue the metaphor, how does your story influence how you will run the race?

In this chapter, we'll take an inventory of the past and

present, looking at how ancestral stories and intangible wealth can be the building blocks of a legacy that is uniquely yours.

THE TRUE MEANING OF WEALTH

It's probably no surprise that the monetary inheritance I received from my parents was quite modest. My parents worked hard and saved what they could, but it was never a large sum of money. And yet, my parents left me immeasurable wealth.

They demonstrated hard work and perseverance. They talked to me about what it took to succeed and how we would have to work that much harder because we were foreigners, starting from scratch and having to prove ourselves. I watched my dad, the manager of a restaurant, mop floors and carry fifty-pound bags of rice up the stairs to the kitchen while also performing other menial tasks to make a living. Seeing this built character within me, so much so that these lessons had a much greater impact on my life than if my parents had left a million dollars in the bank.

I believe that this differentiation between *tangible wealth* and *intangible wealth* is sorely lacking in today's society. We tend to look at our bank accounts or investment portfolios and use that to determine whether or not we're wealthy. But Charles Stanley wrote that true wealth is the ability to enjoy God's blessings,[11] and I agree.

Intangible wealth encompasses a person's spiritual qualities, which are manifested within believers by the power of the Holy Spirit. These qualities characterize a life dedicated to God and include such fruit of the Spirit as "love, joy, peace, patience, kindness, goodness, faithfulness, gentleness, [and] self-control" (Galatians 5:22–23 ESV). Other examples of intangible wealth are a person's time, talent, reputation, faith, and wisdom.

Tangible wealth, on the other hand, refers to money, investments, and material possessions—a person's net worth, if you will. Too often, we focus on tangible wealth when we need to focus on intangible wealth. We wonder why our bank accounts aren't growing and neglect to consider the ways our character is building. We focus on our portfolios, salaries, and net worth when we need to focus on how we treat others, our relationship with God, and our heart for the people around us.

At times, focusing on our intangible wealth translates into riches, but that's not the point. Our heavenly Father's goal is that we live with a Kingdom mindset. His goal is that we obtain and grow our intangible wealth and then pass that wealth along to those around us and to future generations. We need to understand this truth fully if we're going to "get set" to run the race of life.

FOCUS ON YOUR REAL WEALTH

I didn't always understand the importance of intangible wealth. For years, I took the intangible wealth that my parents had passed on to me and applied it to my work in the corporate world. There, it served me well. I got promotions

33

and raises. I succeeded! What I didn't realize was that I had traded the wealth my parents had given me—the character-building lessons they had taught me—for a life of chasing after achievements, recognition, and riches.

The more I climbed the corporate ladder, the more I worked. I missed out on time with my wife and family. I missed sporting events, music recitals, school plays with my children, and so much more. I put in overtime during the week and then came home and worked ten or more hours on the weekends!

This was all because I believed that the most valuable thing I could do was work. Coming from an immigrant family, my work ethic was my identity. It was what differentiated me from my colleagues. I remember looking around a staff meeting at GE. I was the only person of color in the entire room, but I didn't want my ethnicity to be the only thing that set me apart. It occurred to me that I might not be able to outthink these incredibly smart people, but I knew that I could outwork them!

Now, don't get me wrong. A good work ethic is absolutely valuable. It's a solid foundation on which a great legacy can be built—but not at the cost of your relationship with God, your relationship with your family, your time, or your focus on the true legacy goal. I had taken the wealth that my parents had given me, and I'd gone to an extreme.

We live in a culture of extremes. The things that we value become obsessions. If we value tangible wealth, then we're never satisfied with the number in our bank account. We always want more. If we value work, then we never know how to step away from the desk and relax. If we feel the pressure of providing for a family, then it quickly becomes our focus, and we're rarely able to notice the needs of those outside of our family circle.

A life of true value is one that has balance. It's one that values relationships and godly purpose more than money, career, and hobbies. A life of true value builds character, and from that character springs a natural balance of accumulating riches, cultivating relationships, excelling at work, and then pushing all of that out to impact the world around you.

"But Richard! You don't understand my situation! Do you really expect me to spend time in relationship and Kingdom work when it's taking all my effort just to keep my family out of bankruptcy?"

Yes, I do. And that's because I believe that God's hand on your life will help to fill in those blanks that you're struggling to fill on your own. This graph shows how God takes our wealth and riches and, by His grace, increases them, using them to multiply our efforts:

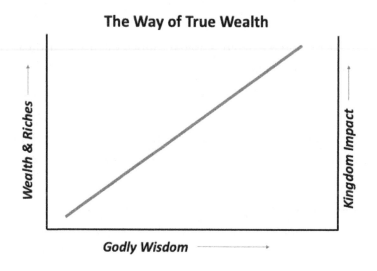

This isn't a get-rich-quick scheme. This isn't a prosperity gospel. It is a focus on what really matters. Unlike prosperity gospels, it begins with godly wisdom and aims to serve God's purposes and desires, not ours, with the resources He entrusts to us. That is how our relationship with God, paired with our intangible wealth and whatever money we have in the bank, can be used for His glory.

But I promise you that He will also take care of you in the process. You will never go without, as promised in 2 Corinthians 9:8, which reads, "Besides, God is able to make every blessing of yours overflow for you, so that in every situation you will always have all you need for any good work" (ISV). Notice that the promise is not that you will have enough to satisfy your own wants and desires. Rather, the promise is that He will give you what you need to be a blessing to others.

This isn't to say that riches are bad or that they aren't worth your time. We already discussed in Chapter One that we are to be caretakers of what God has blessed us with, and part of that involves being smart with our finances and investments. But the goal isn't to hoard treasure. The more you are blessed with wealth and riches, the more of an impact you should be making on the world around you.

YOU'RE ABLE TO IMPACT THE FUTURE

When I was in my twenties and thirties, I never thought to ask myself why God had placed me on this earth. I never thought about my purpose, let alone wondered how I was supposed to serve others. Instead, during those years of my life, I was consumed by my own self-interest. I did what I thought would make me happy, and in America, that comes down to consumerism. I didn't have enough money to travel, but I had enough to enjoy life where I was. *It had never occurred to me to take a step back and ask myself if I was truly living the kind of life that I wanted.*

I found God at twenty-nine (actually, He found me!), and my life changed—but not completely. I found happiness and peace, yet I was still working myself ragged, trying to find my identity in my job and my earthly riches. Then, in my fifties, God tapped me on the shoulder and got me thinking about legacy.

When I first started seriously contemplating legacy, it was mind-blowing to realize that what I did during my life could influence people living decades from now. All my experiences, both good and bad, successes and failures, and whatever wisdom, knowledge, and understanding I'd gained on my life's journey from my parents, other mentors, and growing experiences would eventually become my legacy. I would have an impact on those who came after me—not only through whatever riches or assets I left behind, but more importantly, through the decisions I made, the ways I helped others, and the power of God working through me by His Spirit.

I suddenly felt the weight of the years that I'd spent toiling away at a job and taking care of me and mine. At the same time, I was invigorated by true life meaning. I still had time to make a difference to those around me and those who would come after. God brought to my mind Psalm 102:18: "Write this for the next generation, that a people yet to be created will praise the LORD" (ISV). I want my present life to impact future generations positively for the Kingdom.

Where are you on your journey? Perhaps you feel as though you've wasted some years. Perhaps you need to put your life on pause as you figure out how to hear God's voice. Perhaps you need to give up some things that are important to you, much like I had to give up my obsession with my career.

You might be worried about opening your heart to God and asking Him to take the lead, and I sympathize with that. But I dare you to ask that question anyway. I dare you to step out and choose to make legacy a priority.

Regardless of who you are and how you've lived, your life matters to the people who come after you. Once you decide to stop chasing after tangible wealth and to focus on forming your legacy, you will see the future begin to change.

It starts with family: your spouse, your children, your grandchildren. What you do and how you pour into their lives will have an impact. It will help to shape who they become as they reflect and grow on the foundation that they're given.

When you leave them with a great legacy, they will be empowered to make their own impact. Their lives will affect their children and grandchildren, their co-workers, and their friends. This continuum goes on and on, generation to generation.

YOUR ANCESTRAL STORIES HAVE VALUE

Let me come at it from another angle.

Ancestral stories hold a tremendous amount of wealth. Whether or not you feel that you have any wisdom to offer doesn't matter, because your stories hold wisdom and truth.

At eighteen years old, my dad enlisted in the U. S. Navy to defend a country he was not born in. He served aboard a tank landing ship on D-Day at Normandy. Growing up, my dad was always proud of his service to this great nation, but was the nation proud of him?

Chinese American men and women served in every theater of WWII and sacrificed their lives defending America at a time when the Chinese Exclusion Act of 1882 and its discriminatory practices were in place. The Act, which was on the books for sixty years, prevented non-U. S.-born

Chinese Americans from obtaining U. S. citizenship. Congress declared that Chinese Americans were unfit to be citizens, and their acts of military heroism, bravery, and sacrifice went unrecognized. Despite this, as many as 20,000 Chinese Americans served, 40 percent of them without citizenship. My dad was one of them.

By 2012, sixty-nine years after the Chinese Exclusion Act was repealed, Congress had passed unanimous, bipartisan resolutions that formally expressed regret for the passage of the Act. This was an historic first step Congress took in recognizing the systemic, institutionalized discrimination against Chinese Americans. As a result of a bipartisan bill passed in Congress in 2018, a Congressional Gold Medal was recently awarded posthumously to my dad.

This story is one that has greatly shaped me and my family, but here's the reality of it: I could have heard this story and become bitter. I could have become focused on all of the wrongs done against my family. But my father showed me a different path. You see, my father wasn't bitter. He wasn't resentful. His attitude provided me and my family with a different view of this story.

What happened to my father and other Chinese Americans in this country is horrible, no doubt about it. There rightly should be marches and protests and frustration. But I believe that it's also a story that encourages us to look within our hearts and find love for people who are different from us.

My dad risked his life for a nation that didn't appreciate him. My dad worked hard in a country that stacked the odds against him. He never complained. He always persevered. This attitude has given me and my family incredible wealth.

I thank God that in America, we have the freedom and the opportunity to call out and battle injustices and inequities in our society. I have worked in, lived in, and traveled to six continents, and based on my experiences, there is no country on the face of the earth I prefer to this one. My family is grateful and proud of the sacrifices my father so willingly made for his family and his country. That is how his story has shaped us.

How do your family stories shape you? Do you view them as a source of wealth or a source of pain?

I think of the Irish and the Italians, other groups that came to America and were persecuted and shunned. And of course, I think of the incredible adversity that the Black community has faced and continues to face. Perhaps these cultural stories infuse your own.

I also think of the groups who were the persecutors, the bullies, the slave owners, and the racists. We can glean lessons from their stories, too, as we learn and grow and change.

At the heart of these family histories is identity. You don't have to look very far in today's society to see that there are people walking around with damaged or misplaced identities. People who no longer know who they are. People who lack self-confidence. People who look to earthly pleasures, lifestyles, or ideologies in hopes of finding contentment and happiness.

The answer is found in God and His Son, Jesus Christ. He provides the only identity that matters in the end. You and I are made in the image of God, and we will never be complete until we believe in and accept His Son, Jesus, as our Lord and Savior. You will never be complete until you believe and live this.

I believe that God uses our unique stories to give us a layered identity that only the Creator of the world can give. That's why it's important to dig in and learn our personal histories. Malcolm Gladwell posits in his book *Outliers* that "we pay too much attention to what successful people are like, and too little attention to where they are from: that is, their culture, their family, their generation."[12] We ought to know those who came before us, those whose trials and decisions resulted in the lives we have today. It's about acknowledging the dark stuff, yet focusing on a way forward.

This is the beginning of how we develop family values that are passed from generation to generation and how we shape what makes our family lines unique. It's how we form an identity that goes beyond how we feel today, an identity that is rooted in ancestry.

WHAT MOSES CAN TEACH YOU
ABOUT YOUR LEGACY

In Deuteronomy 11, Moses was in the midst of a farewell address. It was his last message to his people, and in it he chastised them, prophesied, and instructed them for the future. I encourage you to take a few moments to read it.

In this address, Moses tackled some critical ideas about

wealth, values, and legacy. First, Moses summarized over forty years of wilderness wandering by listing the various places the people of Israel had seen and reflecting on the times when they had lacked faith.

When I think of the various places I've lived, there are memories and experiences attached to each physical location. Some of these experiences impacted me in substantial ways. There are locations in my past that represent times of great faith and times of great falling away from my faith. There are places or things that represent great struggle and great blessing, great determination and great frustration.

If we openly consider our past and the various places we've been and lived, we'll see the stories of our lives playing out before us. I think that the Israelites experienced this very thing when Moses talked about everywhere they had been and what had happened there. I think that it caused them to reflect on the good and the bad of their past.

Where have you lived? What locations, cities, and buildings represent your past, and what memories are tied to them? It's important to take a moment to think about those places so you can fully appreciate all that you have been through and what you have learned, both good and bad.

The second thing that Moses tackled in his address was to express his hopes and fears for the people as they were about to enter the Promised Land. Most parents have hopes and fears for their children. Elina and I certainly do. Moses saw the Israelites as his children, and not only did he have hopes and fears for them, but he also wrote those hopes and fears down. He documented them. Perhaps he struggled with what exactly to write. Maybe when he thought about the future, he saw so much promise and hope and also so much that could destroy. He was honest in what he wrote because he knew that his people would depend on it.

The third thing that Moses did in his farewell was to set a bright future for his people, filled with the promises of God, but he was clear that the bright future would only happen if they remained faithful. Moses was writing out his legacy, and God was in the middle of it.

Moses had been with the Israelites for forty years. He knew each one of them intimately. He knew their strengths and weaknesses, and he wanted to give them something that would help them to succeed after he was gone. That's what this farewell address was. There is more to Moses's farewell address, but I believe that those three aspects are most important, and they teach us five valuable lessons:

1. It's important to recount the good and bad experiences of the past. We learn from our experiences, and they help to shape us.

2. It's important to be brutally honest about the past and also about our hopes and fears for the future. If we're not honest about where we came from and what our strengths and weaknesses are, we can't possibly expect to have a great impact on the future.

3. It's important to consider the bigger, God-centered picture. Our lives are so much more than the times when we lapsed in faith. There is a larger story going on, and it's important to recognize that.

4. It's important to reinforce what we've learned by writing it down so that we don't forget and the wisdom is not lost.

5. There are consequences to our actions. While it's true that there is a bigger picture, it's also true that the things we do today have an impact on the things of the future.

Have you talked with your family about the bright future that God has promised all of us if we remain faithful and we live His legacy here on earth? As we talk about our past and our present and how we can use our lives to effect change in future generations, we're creating what's called an *ethical will*. This is exactly what Moses's farewell address was.

WRITE ANOTHER WILL?

Writing an ethical will and passing it from one generation to the next is an ancient Jewish custom in which parents would write a letter to their children that encapsulated everything they had experienced, everything they had learned, and also their hopes and fears for their children's future. These wills included amazing family stories and generations-old wisdom. They contained family values and both wonderful and challenging memories. The goal of these wills was to arm the next generation with the power of the past, to take the lessons learned and the wisdom gained and use them to make the future a better, brighter place.

I want you to consider your own ethical will. I want you

to write down the things that are most important to you, the things you have learned from family members and from your own experiences. This can include stories of the past and advice for the future. Here are some prompts to consider:

- Crucial stories about my parents, grandparents, great-grandparents, and past generations are...

- Our family traditions are...

- The events that have had the greatest impact on my life are...

- The biggest lessons that I've learned are...

- The most difficult time in my life was when...

- The time God surprised me the most was when...

- The role that God has played in my life is...

- My biggest regret is...

- My beliefs are...

- My values are...

- My hopes for my children are...

- My hopes for my grandchildren are...

Most people I talk to have never heard of ethical wills, but I believe that putting one together now, even if you end up reshaping it over time, can help to bring focus to the kind of legacy you want to have today and the kind of legacy you want to leave behind. Too often, we focus on the riches of this world, but ethical wills show us how to focus on the wealth that truly shapes our lives and future generations.

This is how you move to your mark to run the race. This is how you take the desire that you have to leave a legacy and form it into something that can truly make a difference. It starts when you shift your focus from riches to intangible wealth. It continues when you dig up family stories, family values, and ancestral truths. And it ends with an ethical will that, with God's help, will make you unstoppable once it's time to *get set* and then *GO* in the race of life.

Chapter Two Notes

CHAPTER THREE

A Personal Mission Statement

Do not conform to the pattern of this world, but be transformed by the renewing of your mind. Then you will be able to test and approve what God's will is—his good, pleasing and perfect will.

—Romans 12:2 *(NIV)*

When runners take their marks, they do so with a clear idea of how they plan to run the race. They know their own strengths and weaknesses. They know when it's best for them to sprint and when they need to run at a steady, long-distance pace. Just like these runners, we should have a plan to run the race set before us. We should know our unique skills and giftings, and we should know how God wants to use them for His glory.

Knowing yourself and what God has called you to do while running the race of life is the final component to this first phase of the process, which I like to refer to as the self-preparation phase. In this chapter, I'm going to help you discover your unique mission.

FIND YOUR PURPOSE

What mission has God given you? How has He uniquely gifted you to enter into radical generosity and create a legacy that lasts long after you're gone?

If you're like most people, you're scratching your head at these questions. You may have a loose handle on your personal calling and purpose on this earth, but if pressed to get into the details, you'd come up empty-handed.

This is the part of the process where we dig into those details, and I believe that a big component of this discovery process lies within a personal mission statement. To zero in on your passions, dreams, strengths, and goals and figure out your unique role in God's kingdom, a mission statement is crucial.

If you don't already have a personal mission statement, you are closer to one than you may think. I've written at length about the importance of keeping God at the center of this process. Everything begins and ends with Him. He is our Creator, after all, and He knows the role that each of us is meant to play in bringing His kingdom to the earth.

Connecting with God should begin to give you a sense of who you are, what you're about, and how He wants to use you. From there, you will consider your hopes, dreams, and ambitions. All of this will come together to create a meaningful, impactful mission statement that will guide your life going forward.

If you don't declare who you are and the role that you play in God's kingdom work, you'll leave yourself open for others to fill in the blanks. When I was growing up, my immigrant parents taught my siblings and me to persevere, keep our heads down, and work hard. We weren't encouraged to speak out or cause problems, even in the face of discrimination and bullying. This approach fit what America expected from Asian Americans ever since the 1880s. It's only recently that the Asian American community has begun breaking the mold, speaking up, and saying, "We won't be silent anymore!" We are taking control of our personal mission statements, so to speak. We won't let others define that for us any longer.

How has the world around you put you inside a box? How has the narrative about who you are and what you're capable of prevented you from growing into your true identity as a child of God? More importantly, how has your own lack of action prevented you from living your best legacy?

Andy Stanley says, "It's your direction, not your intention, that determines your destination."[13] God is our anchor, and by His grace, He gives direction to our lives. But—and this is important—He also grants us the freedom to decide how we choose to live and how we will use the resources He has given us. The choice is yours.

The North Star in the Northern Hemisphere remains in the same location every night from dusk to dawn. It's unmoving. It's constant. And sailors have used it to navigate waters for hundreds of years.

Your mission statement can be your North Star, keeping you on course and always pointing to your true purpose. It will help you to focus on what you should be doing today. It will help your decision-making. If God's Spirit is prompting you to change course, your personal mission statement will help you with that, offering clarity on which direction to take and how to adjust your momentum.

You can use your mission statement as a guide to assess a myriad of potential choices. I visit my mission statement frequently, and I use it to determine which opportunities are in alignment with the mission God has given me. I use it to gauge my thoughts and ideas, ensuring that I'm pursuing the right things. It has become an invaluable tool, and I believe that it's crucial to running this race well, which is exactly why I'd love for you to try your hand at crafting your own personal mission statement.

Go "Where No Man Has Gone Before"

I want you to dream big when it comes to your mission statement. I want you to "boldly go"[14] where you never would have dreamed you'd go.

During my forty-two years in the corporate world, I've been involved in numerous exercises to develop vision and mission statements for various companies. Many of these meetings were tedious and lengthy. We'd spend endless hours wordsmithing and picking apart the difference between vision statements and mission statements. This is not how I recommend you go about the process! One of my all-time favorite mission statements is not one I helped to develop. See if you can recognize it:[15]

Space: the final frontier. These are the voyages of the starship *Enterprise*. Its five-year mission: to explore strange new worlds. To seek out new life and new civilizations. To boldly go where no man has gone before!

I became a Trekkie in 1969 when *Star Trek* hit the television screen. At the start of each episode, William Shatner would recite the mission of the starship *Enterprise* while the show's unmistakable musical score played in the background.

I absolutely love this mission statement, and I encourage you to use it as inspiration as you write yours. One reason it stands out to me is because it's time-bound. This mission would last for five years, at which point they would recalibrate and possibly start a new mission. As we work on our mission statements, it's important to recognize the role that time will play. The season of life you are in right now will not last forever, and the goals and tasks that are important now will not always need your attention. So as you write, keep in mind that a mission statement is not forever. It needs to be revised and rewritten as life changes.

Another reason the Star Trek mission statement works well is because while it focuses on the task at hand (planetary exploration), it also leaves things a bit open-ended. Their ultimate quest is to find new things, whether that be planets, people, other lifeforms, cultures—anything they come across that is new and unfamiliar. That leaves a lot of wiggle room when it comes to how they pursue their exploration goal.

Lastly, this mission statement stands out because of the brazen nature of the last line: "To boldly go where no man has gone before." It reminds me of 2 Timothy 1:7, which reads, "For God has not given us a spirit of fear and timidity, but of power, love, and self-discipline" (NLT).

As you think about your mission statement, consider how you can maintain a sense of adventure. God has the details under control. It's up to you simply to *GO*.

"Your Mission, Should You Choose to Accept It"

Search me, God, and know my heart; test me and know my anxious thoughts. See if there is any offensive way in me, and lead me in the way everlasting.
—Psalm 139:23–24 *(NIV)*

It's time to begin writing.

As you'd probably expect, if you Google "personal mission statement," there are hundreds of thousands of search results. The last time I checked, a simple Amazon search turned up over 1,000 results for books on personal mission statements. That's 1,000 opinions on how to do this. What does that tell me? There really isn't a right or wrong way! The most important thing is that you find an approach that works for you.

Some time ago, I came across a straightforward, well-written guide by Andy Andrews entitled *Your Personal Mission Statement Action Plan*. In it, Andrews asked three simple but profound questions:[16]

> 1. Who am I? (What are you all about? What is your role as steward?)
>
> 2. Who am I becoming? (What are your life goals? What is important to you?)
>
> 3. What is my purpose in life? (God uniquely created you for a purpose—what is it?)

I love the simplicity of this approach. A mission statement doesn't describe who you've been for the last ten years; it describes who you are now and who you want to become. It looks to the future, to your legacy.

Some things to keep in mind as you begin to form your mission statement are:

1. Keep it short. One sentence is ideal. Remember that this is *your* mission statement. The words you use are there to guide *you*, not to impress someone else. It's about being true and obedient to God.

2. Name the groups you want to impact and those you love.

3. Be bold enough to share your mission statement with others to solicit feedback.

4. Don't strive for perfection. Consider it a living mission statement that can be shaped and revised over

time as you grow and as God reveals more to you about His plan for your life. At the very least, make a point to revisit your statement on an annual basis.

5. Make sure that it's meaningful to you. It has to be meaningful to you before it can be meaningful to someone else.

The Apostle Paul wrote, "Examine yourselves to see whether you are in the faith; test yourselves. Do you not realize that Christ Jesus is in you—unless, of course, you fail the test?" (2 Corinthians 13:5 NIV). Sincere introspection is part of the Christian walk. It's the only way to get to the bottom of our bad habits, improper actions, impure thoughts, and wrong attitudes. That's why this process is so important. We have access to a loving and all-powerful God who will provide us with forgiveness, help, encouragement, and the means to confess our shortcomings and move forward in life with hope. In other words, if you begin this process earnestly, with a sincere heart, God will meet you there and carry you through.

GET PERSONAL

To passionately leverage my faith, wisdom, and possessions to inspire, influence, and aid my family, the church, and the needy.

The above is my mission statement. I don't share it to boast or to show off, but to give you a glimpse into where this process will lead you. This statement represents me perfectly, as I take 1 Peter 4:10 to heart: "Each of you should use whatever gift you have received to serve others, as faithful stewards of God's grace in its various forms" (NIV).

I chose these words intentionally. I chose "to passionately leverage" because I know that if I'm not passionate about something, I won't be able to keep it going. I won't be able to sustain it. So passion is important for me.

I chose "my faith, wisdom, and possessions" because I believe that these are blessings I've been given that reflect my life experience as a whole.

I chose "to inspire, influence, and aid my family, the church, and the needy" because that is broad enough to allow me to enter into ministry wherever and however God leads me. I am most passionate about having an outsized impact on "family, church, and the needy."

Anyone who knows me can see that I've strived to be obedient to and consistent with this mission statement. They can see how I've taken my years of real-world experience and turned it into ministry. They can see my passion in the nonprofit-organization boards on which I serve and my intentionality in the opportunities I say yes to and the ones I turn down.

That may seem like a lot of impact based on one mission statement, and it's true. I believe that even as a mission statement gives you a framework for who you are and how God can use you, it also provides you with freedom. My mission statement gives me the freedom to aid my family, the church, and the needy however I see fit. If I want to serve on a ministry board for homeless people, I can do that. If I want to serve on a board for pregnancy services, I can do that. There is freedom in following Jesus.

Allow me to offer some insight into how I form my mission statement. (Refer to the template used earlier in the chapter as needed.) First, I consider, *"Who am I?"* I am a child of God, created to love and serve Him. I serve Him through serving others. I am uniquely made, and through all my life experiences, good and not so good, I have been directed to accomplish His purpose on earth.

Second, I ask, *"What am I becoming?"* I shared earlier that throughout my professional life, I was committed to climbing the corporate ladder. The more success I had, the more committed I was to my job and profession, even at the expense of my family and faith. Sure, I enjoyed an enriched church life, and I was growing in the Lord, but the amount of time I put into my job was unhealthy. It was an idol in my life. God held me and my family together through that time, and He brought me out of it. I've made peace with God, and He has allowed me to make up for the years lost. He has even given me the opportunity to use what I learned in the corporate world to serve nonprofits today!

Some ways to grow in the right direction are:

- Learn how to be a more generous person.

- Learn how to demonstrate generosity.

- Learn how to be more open to the leading of the Holy Spirit concerning how you can be more effective in doing Kingdom work.

This is not an exhaustive list, but those key elements have transformed my life and helped me to become the person I am today.

Third, I ask, *"What is my purpose?"* My purpose is to inspire, influence, and aid. Here are some examples of what this has looked like at various points in my life:

- Mentoring a newly ordained pastor.

- Coaching a newly appointed executive director of the local rescue mission.

- Joining the board of a newly formed nonprofit that intends to transform the local business community through Christ, one leader at a time.

- Joining the board of a Christian foundation whose mission is to mobilize resources by inspiring biblical generosity.

- Providing leadership to our family foundation, the Two Tunics Legacy Fund. Our mission is to live out and promote the call to action in Luke 3:11. We do this by engaging, challenging, and partnering with others to demonstrate visibly the power of God's provision and compassion to a world in need.

- Promoting generosity in our sphere of influence through group discussion and focused Bible studies.

I don't put each of these in my mission statement; that would be far too confining. Rather, my statement allows room for these activities that have come naturally from my past experience—not only from my corporate history, but also from God placing opportunities, people, and circumstances in my path. Each of these fits perfectly with who God has created me to be. My mission statement and how I live it out may change slightly over time, but the core of it stays the same.

Finally, to ensure that my mission statement fits God's call on my life, I share it with others. I choose one or two people who know me well and who will be honest with me, and I ask for their insight. These conversations are so valuable, as they help me to identify what I might be missing. Sharing my mission statement with others also keeps me accountable. It keeps me on track. If I take an opportunity that isn't in line with my mission statement, the people who see that can help me get back on track.

NOW IT'S YOUR TURN

Crafting a mission statement may take longer than you think. It requires commitment and intentionality, but it is so worth it! Your mission statement will quickly become your North Star, allowing you to say no with ease to the things that don't line up with your legacy calling while helping you to identify the opportunities that do line up with what you're about.

This is how you prepare for the race. This is how you train

yourself to be ready and capable as you lead your family toward legacy-minded living.

A quote attributed to Abraham Lincoln says, "You cannot escape the responsibility of tomorrow by evading it today."[17] So take an afternoon (or a week, if needed) and start crafting your mission statement. Listen for anything the Holy Spirit has to say to you about it. You'll be surprised by what God will reveal to you in this process. When you are finished with your personal mission statement, you'll be ready to "take your mark" in preparation for the race ahead.

Chapter Three Notes

PART TWO: GET SET

It's Not Just About You

One generation shall praise thy works to another, and shall declare thy mighty acts.

—Psalm 145:4 *(KJV)*

You've taken your mark. Now it's time to *get set*.

As we've discussed in previous chapters, the Legacy Continuum isn't about a single contribution. It's not about my individual legacy or about yours. Rather, the Legacy Continuum is about collective legacy. It's about how our parents and grandparents helped to shape who we are and what we value. It's about the stories of our ancestry and our identity as children of God. All of these things come together to form our living legacy. After we're gone, our legacy will continue making a difference in the lives of future generations.

It's true that any one person can make an impact on his or her family's legacy, but it takes a team effort for that impact to take full effect and reach its full potential. God never meant for this to be a lonely sprint to the finish line. Think of it more like a relay race.

Your family members have an equally important role to play, and it's time to invite them to join the race. As you "get set" together, you'll learn how to prepare your team for your mission in the Legacy Continuum.

In this chapter, we're going to discuss how to welcome family members to the legacy team, how you can connect them to the past, and how to forge a path to the future together.

WE'RE BETTER TOGETHER

God wants us to be in community. He never intended us to shoulder the weight of His call alone. We see this exemplified in the early church. After Jesus ascended, the church banded together. They did life together and shared possessions (Acts 4:32–35). They shouldered one another's burdens (Galatians 6:2) and met together, encouraging one another (Hebrews 10:24–25).

Most importantly, we know that God is with those who gather in His name (Matthew 18:20). Coming together in community is not only part of His plan, but also an incredible way to commune with Him. If God called the church to come together as the above verses dictate, how much more should we come together as a family?

The Legacy Continuum was meant to be supported by an entire team of runners, not by any one person's solo effort. The sooner your family joins the team and enters into this race with you, the more effective and meaningful your legacy journey will be.

So, how do you form your team? The best rule of thumb is to follow your instincts and to pray—a lot! Your team could include your spouse, children, in-laws, grandchildren, siblings, parents, grandparents—anyone whom you cannot imagine running this race without.

Understand that it may not appeal to everyone at the beginning, but don't let that cause you to give up easily. Think of this as a process. You may not get everyone on board at the outset, but you need to have a plan to persevere when bringing the outliers into the fold. It may take a little longer with some than others. Your daughter-in-law may be a great fit while your son would rather sit it out—and that's okay! You can always have different levels of partnership. You can have a core group that meets regularly and an annual gathering to fill in the rest of the family.

The main goal is to be flexible, understanding, and patient while also remaining committed to forming your team and becoming intentional about legacy. After all, this is not just about you. You want a team that you can count on to run the race with vigor, a team that will chase after legacy.

HOW DO YOU TRAIN YOUR TEAM?

Train up a child in the way he should go: and when he is old, he will not depart from it.
—Proverbs 22:6 *(KJV)*

Of course, there will be a learning curve. Taking these intentional steps with your team may challenge your leadership capabilities, and your team will need to be trained in what this different approach to life entails.

Merriam-Webster defines *train* as "to teach so as to make fit, qualified, or proficient; to form by instruction, discipline, or drill; to make prepared (as by exercise) for a test of skill."[18] By that very definition, training someone is not an easy task. It requires commitment and follow-through, care and understanding. At the same time, it can be one of the most rewarding things a person ever does. Seeing a child, student, or friend go from ignorance to understanding is a powerful thing!

As with most things in life, getting started is always a challenge. When I first started holding regular family legacy meetings with my children and wife, my goal was to get them excited about legacy. I wanted us to be all-in, pursuing this together, each operating within his or her strengths. Still, in the beginning, I remember feeling as though I was the only person who wanted to be there.

We'd meet quarterly, and I'd talk and talk. My family would listen, but I didn't know how they were receiving what I was sharing. Five years went by before I finally felt as though we were aligned and engaged as a group. Five years! That's a long time to wait for your team to get on board, but as I look back on that time, I realize that I went about it the wrong way. I didn't seek their input. I didn't ask for their ideas. I focused too much on my agenda instead of opening up the discussion. I failed to remember that this is not just about me.

Ecclesiastes 11:9 reads, "Rejoice, O young man, in your youth, and let your heart cheer you in the days of your youth. Walk in the ways of your heart and the sight of your eyes. But know that for all these things God will bring you into judgment" (ESV). This is such a good reminder that as parents, we shouldn't get too serious or overbearing when it comes to teaching our children. It's important that we give freedom, that we allow kids to be kids, as the saying goes. Of course, the harder lesson is for parents to help our kids learn about individual accountability—that there are consequences to our actions.

I pressed on. I kept tweaking things, kept adjusting how I engaged with my family on the topics of time, talent, and treasure. I tried different approaches and angles. And like drops in a sea, the ripples finally made their way to shore. My children began asking questions, discussion deepened, and we came to a point where we were open and honest about some of the struggles each of us faced. What started out as a difficult process marred by uncertainty eventually developed into something beautiful and effective. As the years went on, the team came together.

I think about track and field. You won't come off the starting block perfectly every time. Every once in a while, you'll stumble, or your timing will be off. Things won't go according to your plan. Your optimistic vision of your family meeting may not unfold quite the way you see it in your head and the way you want it to be in your heart, but it is worth the investment. Although everything may not go according to your plan, be comforted by the knowledge that God is working in the background. The result will be something beyond anything you imagined or planned by yourself.

JUMP-START YOUR LEGACY

It may feel as though you're navigating this alone, but did you know that you've been given a jump-start from the past?

I vaguely remember my very first high school track team meeting, but I do remember the coach talking about the senior tracksters who had just graduated. He waxed on and on about their stellar accomplishments and the records they amassed, both as a team and as individuals. Though I struggled as a teenager to believe that I could be just as good as the students whom the coach talked about, his stories were inspiring, and his excitement was motivational.

Our coach was passing on the legacy that we were inheriting, a legacy that would not only push us to achieve even greater results, but also instill within us a sense of pride in our team and school. It's no wonder that at a citywide track meet, I could almost feel the confidence oozing from the top teams as they strutted onto the field. They were propelled by their team legacies, and I'm sure that we brought our own air of confidence as we took our places.

It's no different with a multi-generational legacy. Whether we realize it or not, those before us have helped to set the course of our lives. The legacy that you inherited, even if it's less than ideal, should motivate you to be better, and your relationship with Christ should arm you with what you need to make your own impact with the family members you have around you. Again, remember that it's not just about you.

STORIES ARE POWERFUL

Your legacy will provide your children and those who follow them a connection to those who preceded them. I've talked a lot about legacy in terms of family stories that are passed down from generation to generation, but why is the act of sharing these stories so valuable?

According to a survey done by StoryTerrace, 45 percent of adult children learn more about their parents from discovering photos and family possessions than direct conversations with them.[19] Why do you think that is? It could be that these discussions are difficult or that the past is too painful.

When my dad received a Congressional Gold Medal of Honor, I gave each of my children a replica. I want them to remember what he did and who he was, and that memento is part of his legacy.

We have pictures of us as a family riding camels in the Gobi Desert. We have souvenirs from our various trips around the world, rugs from Persia and India and Turkey. My wife has jewelry that she will pass down to my daughters. Each piece has its own unique story, and some of it has very old ties to the family.

We have photo books, boxes of mementos, and art on the walls. All of these things are visual representations of our family legacy. They represent memories, experiences, and people. They represent us.

My house is a museum of the life that we have lived together. We haven't made our final decisions on how we will divide it all up once we are gone from this world, but the memories and stories of our family permeate everything with meaning. The power of exploring our family stories is that our children will gain a better understanding of who they are and how they were molded in their formative years. This knowledge will serve to empower them in their lives moving forward.

What do you have that represents the legacy you have built as a family? What were the shared experiences that you will never forget? What memories have yet to be created?

You don't have to travel the world or buy jewelry to have tokens of your family's story. When my parents were near the end of life, I wanted more than family stories. I wanted to understand what they were thinking and how they made key life decisions. I craved this valuable information to gain deeper insight into the person I wanted to be throughout my life. Communicating this type of insight to your family is priceless and can happen every day over the course of your shared lives.

Spend time together exploring a city or town where you grew up, maybe visiting a park that holds particular meaning for you. Go through a box that's been sitting in the attic. Discover—or perhaps rediscover—your legacy. I guarantee that it's closer and easier to find than you think.

Face the Past with Vulnerability

As you explore your family legacy together, seeking out answers and information, you'll discover how the past has informed the present. More importantly, you'll find that it will also inform the future, if you allow it.

While this process of exploration and discovery can be beneficial, it can also be uncomfortable. Mindsets, values, and creeds from the past can sometimes impact future family members. This is why vulnerability and honesty are so important when exploring your family legacy.

When it came to my dad, I didn't begin to ask him questions about the past until he was near the end of his life. Perhaps it was my own fear of vulnerability that got in the way of me exploring my family history with my dad. It's a difficult thing to look at the past and see how it has affected the present.

On one occasion, I asked my dad what went through his mind when his parents told him that they were permanently sending him to the U. S. at age fifteen. Can you imagine? He had no knowledge of the English language or American culture. However, my dad told me that his only thought was to be obedient to his parents' wishes.

This response surprised me and also shed light on why he was so strict while I was growing up. He would not tolerate any disobedience or backtalk. His parenting method was molded after what he knew as a child, and it impacted me as a father, too. Looking back, I can see that I was strict with my daughters when they were growing up. My father's legacy had become my legacy, and this particular aspect of our legacy wasn't ideal!

Family stories are impactful, and the lessons they teach us can inform the future. To grow from the lessons of the past, we need to be vulnerable with one another. I've certainly admitted to my family that I haven't always been the best father or husband. My attitude wasn't always right, and I didn't always reflect the Bible's command to love your wife (Ephesians 5:25).

By revealing my vulnerabilities, I have been able to show my children that I'm an incredibly flawed person and that I want to be better. Engaging in this conversation shows that I want to change. I want a new legacy for our family because it's not just about me.

It would be easy for me to approach family legacy the way I operated in the corporate world, where the buck stopped with me. It would be easy for me to take a dictatorial approach and require my family to live and act a certain way so that our family legacy looks the way I want it to look. In our early family meetings about legacy, I tried that route. I did the talking. I cast the vision. It was me, me, me.

But this isn't about dictating how other people are to live their lives. It's not about filling their heads with more rules. Rather, it's about providing a venue for them to share, to talk, to be vulnerable. This is about taking the past, learning from it, and using those lessons to craft an ongoing story *together* that will make life better and more meaningful for future generations.

I believe that by being open and vulnerable, we encourage

curiosity in our children. By creating a safe space for them to ask questions, we are more likely to engage in meaningful dialogue. I believe that children, especially adult children, have a natural curiosity about their heritage and ancestry. It shouldn't take much effort to enter into those discussions with them.

Start by going through an old photo album or walking through a family tree together. Invite the grandparents to be part of this process, if possible, and make it a fun day of stories and memories. It's important to establish a habit of setting aside family time. This practice of connecting as a family and reminiscing on family stories should be regular and ongoing.

THE BLESSING OF LEGACY

Ultimately, the goal in all of this is to make room for a life of blessing for our children and our children's children. Of course, the concept of blessing can be a bit squishy.

Many would say that the blessings they wish upon their children include good health, prosperity, fulfillment, and wealth. There's certainly nothing wrong with those, but when I did a brief study on the word *blessing*, I found that the Bible has a different definition.

Biblical blessing is God's power and enablement to accomplish His will for your life. In other words, God blesses us with the things we need to participate in fulfilling His will on earth. Another critical aspect of blessing is that the things that come from God will always grow and multiply, often in ways we don't expect. In other words, the return on our meager investment of time, talent, and treasure will yield results that will far exceed our expectations.

When you look at this concept as a whole, you will realize that God's blessings are not to be kept for our benefit. They should be dispensed to others. We are blessed to be a blessing to others.

Of course, I ask God for health and prosperity and all of those good things for my children and grandchildren, but I now realize that His blessing may not include any of those benefits. The most important blessing they could receive is to know who they are in Christ and for that to propel them to enter into what He wants to do in them and through them.

I believe that when we gather as a family and consider our stories of the past and present, we are better able to enter into what God has for us in the here and now. We are better equipped to receive true blessing from Him, the blessing to accomplish His will, and it will impact our family lines and the world for generations to come.

This is why the race was never meant to be run alone. I think of Hebrews 12:1, which reads: "Therefore, since we are surrounded by so great a cloud of witnesses, let us also lay aside every weight, and sin which clings so closely, and let us run with endurance the race that is set before us" (ESV).

This journey is not about one single person making a difference. It's about your family coming together and choosing now to live for a better future, the future that God has for them.

Chapter Four Notes

Understanding Team Dynamics

Yes, the body has many different parts, not just one part.
—1 Corinthians 12:14 (NLT)

When it comes to track and field, there is nothing more exciting than watching an experienced, well-coached relay team pass the baton from one runner to the next seamlessly, without breaking stride.

It goes without saying that speed matters—that's a given—but in a relay race, the fastest team does not always win. Rather, the team that is the best at passing the baton is usually the one that ends up on top.

Passing the baton is no simple task. Imagine being at top speed, sweaty, tired, and having to hand the baton to a fresh runner who is eager to maintain the momentum. It's no surprise that sweaty hands, a lack of coordination between the runners, the pressure of competition, and distractions from the stands can result in botched handoffs or, even worse, a dropped baton, which results in immediate disqualification.

If that isn't enough pressure, it's the relay race that often determines the winning team for that day's entire track-and-field meet. In a tight competition, if the track-and-field team can work together skillfully to win the relay race, the team will be positioned to win the entire competition.

A relay race requires understanding which team member plays which role and leaning on each person's strength for the best outcome, and the same goes for you and your team. The success of your Legacy Continuum will depend on your team's ability to work together.

What Makes a Winning Team?

When my high school track team trained for the 4 x 400-meter relay race, we spent very little time improving our running skills. Instead, we focused on mastering the art of baton passing. We practiced and experimented with various techniques. We spent time learning how to work together and encourage one another, and we agreed on a strategy. Our coach worked with us extensively, finding out each person's strengths and weaknesses and how best to position each team member in the lineup. You see, we already knew how to run. We just needed to learn how to run together.

The same goes for your legacy journey. The first step of "On Your Mark" is critical because that's where you learn how to run this particular race. You learn about the importance of legacy and how the Legacy Continuum fits

God's plan for your life. Once you've had that training, it's time to learn how to "Get Set" and bring your family, your team, onto the track. Each team member will need to learn how to pass the baton and how to maximize your team's efforts.

Within your family's Legacy Continuum, the baton represents all that you intend to pass on to future generations. It encompasses both your tangible riches, or economic resources, and your intangible wealth, which includes your beliefs, morals, values, and memories. The baton ensures that your contribution to the Legacy Continuum won't simply vanish at the end of your life. If you've prepared your team properly, your particular legacy will endure for multiple generations. Just think about that! You can be a voice in someone's life without ever meeting that person.

This is a truly beautiful thing because it gives real purpose to the lessons you've learned, the hardships you've faced, and the revelations God has given you along the way. It ensures that your contribution to the world will endure and reach many more people. You have it within your power to inspire the future with the past.

The baton does not require someone with a perfect life. Whether you consider your life a rousing success or a total failure, your life is replete with stories, and those stories contain wisdom that has immense value. The baton is the keeper of those stories, and what's even more amazing is that others can add to it.

Imagine pouring all that you know into this baton and then passing it to the next person, who does the same and then passes it on to the next person, who also contributes. That smooth transfer of wisdom and knowledge from one person to the next is what creates a multiplying effect. Passing the baton will have an outsized impact on your Legacy Continuum.

In addition to the baton, team dynamics are a crucial component of success in a relay race. As a team member, I was expected to run the fastest leg I was capable of and flawlessly pass and receive the baton within the designated exchange zone. Even if I successfully received and handed off the baton and I outran everyone else in my leg, my team could still lose the race if others on my team didn't perform their roles as well. This is what makes running a relay race so exciting and so heartbreaking at the same time.

In building a Legacy Continuum, the finish line is inconsequential. There is no finish line until Jesus returns and establishes a new heaven and a new earth. What matters is how your team works together to ensure a clean legacy handoff from generation to generation.

When coaches assemble a relay team, they assess the individual abilities of each runner. They determine roles within the team based on how each team member handles the baton and runs. I've witnessed firsthand how some runners will put a death grip on the baton, even to the point of hampering their running technique. I've seen other runners who are so cavalier with the baton that they're constantly dropping it, even in mid-stride. Meanwhile, the good runners appear to be oblivious to the baton's presence. It's an extension of their bodies.

Individual personalities also come into play. Some runners perform better under pressure, and they're at their best when they're making up lost ground. Others perform at their peak when they're in the lead. Indeed, an adept coach will try new things and mix up the team rotation in the hopes of finding the most effective combination and order of runners for each relay race.

How does this help you in preparing your family for their legacy journey? After all, in life, we don't get to choose our family members. What a family does offer is a unique gathering of strengths and abilities. When preparing your team for their legacy journey, you don't have to fit anyone forcibly into a particular event, cause, or mission. Instead, you can match the mission to your team, choosing what to pursue based on the unique strengths of your team members. You get to define the type of race that you're going to run.

Elina, my wife, is the natural skeptic of the family. She is the one to ask questions and seek clarification. She can anticipate worst-case scenarios.

My daughter Vanessa is a big-picture person and very goal-oriented. She is constantly driving for action and commitment.

My daughter Vivian is our neutral sounding board. She prefers to hear all sides before committing, and she often brings up things we haven't thought of.

Like Vanessa, I am a big-picture person and one to drive the team forward, but I also have a responsibility to draw on everyone's strengths so that we arrive at the best possible solution.

With two Type A personalities on the same team, we tend to push for timely decisions and action. We need Elina to slow us down, and we need to hear Vivian's thoughtful perspective to show us things that we wouldn't have considered on our own.

Each person on my team brings valuable strengths, and I have learned (and am still learning) how to lean into those strengths for maximum impact. After my wife and I are gone, our daughters will take the baton and prepare our grandchildren to receive it. They will form their own unique team of personalities and strengths, so they will need to be willing to adapt. They'll need to make adjustments so that the baton isn't dropped.

Understanding the dynamics of your team will ensure that your baton will be passed from generation to generation, resulting in maximum Kingdom impact.

CULTIVATE YOUR TEAM FOR RADICAL GENEROSITY

We don't always have the ability to choose who is on our family team, but we certainly have the ability to develop a plan that caters to our strengths. What are your team's strengths? What does each person bring? We can develop roles and responsibilities that allow each member to shine.

This means learning to balance the creative extrovert with the thoughtful introvert. It means knowing who would be the best person to document your meetings and who would be the best person to organize action. Identifying your team members' individual strengths will better position you to run the race well. Knowing each individual team member will also position you to develop a vision for each person.

As you focus on laying a foundation for each member of your team to thrive, keep in mind that the ultimate goal of living a life of radical generosity is for the perpetual benefit of generations to come. I recommend that you reflect on the following questions to help you be intentional in your efforts.

1. What are your prayers and dreams for your children, grandchildren, and beyond? As you nurture your team and decide what goals will fit you all best, I've found that an effective way to move forward is to think about the prayers and dreams that you have for your children, grandchildren, and continuing generations after you're gone.

There are scriptures I use to guide these prayers. First, I consider 1 Chronicles 29:19, in which David asked God that his son Solomon would maintain an upright heart and that he would continue the work that David had started. I pray this for my family line. Then I ask God for wisdom, praying Proverbs 4:11–13, which reminds us that wisdom is essential to lasting legacy.

I also look at Hebrews 12:7–11, which reminds me not to become content with the progress I've made, but rather to seek godly discipline so that I may be continually transformed to resemble more closely the righteousness of Jesus. I pray this for myself and my children, and I pray that my progeny will never waiver from their faith (1 Corinthians 16:13).

I pray that they will do the right thing (Proverbs 10:9), and I pray for God's favor upon them, even when they make mistakes (Psalm 103:13). Unlike my ancestors, who remained silent despite all the injustices they suffered, I want my progeny to speak out against injustice and to be bold in all they do, claiming Deuteronomy 1:30: "The LORD your God who goes before you will himself fight for you" (ESV).

From these scriptures, I have formed specific prayer requests for the future of my family's legacy. When I look at these requests, I am reminded again of my track coach. Even though I was a mediocre runner, he never put undue pressure on me to perform beyond my natural abilities. He simply wanted me to be at my very best, whatever that looked like. He was after progress, not perfection, and that is the heart that I now have for my family.

Here are some of the things I pray for regarding how my team will work together toward a quality Legacy Continuum:

- That each generation will experience greater success than the last. That they will find ways of being insanely generous and have an even greater impact on the Kingdom than I could ever imagine.

- That the runners will stay in the same lane, that they will be of one mind and work toward a common goal. In a relay race, one step outside the lane results in immediate disqualification. Similarly, when it comes to the Legacy Continuum, time spent pursuing other things, even good things, that don't move your team toward the goal is time lost.

- That they will act swiftly and decisively to make progress. While major decisions shouldn't be rushed, there should be an urgency to move forward, because withholding critical aid to the poor and helpless can have life-and-death implications.

- That they will cheer one another on. Much like a relay team encourages and cheers the last runner to the finish line, I want my descendants to support one another and be there for one another despite any disagreements that will undoubtedly occur.

These prayers have helped to shape a vision for my legacy decades after I'm gone, and they are invaluable tools to help me discern how today's team should operate. If a goal or strategy doesn't line up with these future dreams and goals, then I know that we're getting off track.

2. How can you connect your children's dreams to generosity and legacy? Of course, *my* dreams for my family's legacy aren't the only ones that matter. Elina's, Vivian's, and Vanessa's dreams also play a vital role in the work that we do. My wife and daughters have unique and worthy desires, and if I can't find a way to fit them into what we do together, then eventually my team will lose interest and do their own thing.

How have I been able to bring the dreams and passions of my individual family members into the idea of our family legacy? There are a few things I've done that have seemed to work well. Of course, I'm no parenting expert! What works for me may not work for you, but in the spirit of transparency, here is how I have helped my daughters to connect their interests with our family goal of generosity and legacy.

First, I talk with them. Asking them about the causes that they are passionate about and the issues that tug at their heartstrings is the most direct and sometimes the easiest way to uncover how their individual interests could fit within the family legacy.

I have also exposed them to volunteer work. One Thanksgiving, I invited my two daughters, my son-in-law, and my eleven-year-old grandson to volunteer serving Thanksgiving meals to the homeless. While the adults were the servers, my grandson bused the tables and spent quality time with many homeless folks. We had a chance afterward to discuss his experience, and I cannot help but feel that it had a profound impact on him. This was a way to get him and other members of my family thinking about generosity and how they could use their time, talent, and treasure to help others.

Another approach that I utilize is to be a living example to my children. "Do as I say, not as I do" is a common parenting phrase—and I have certainly used it when frustrated—but it runs counter to what we are trying to achieve with legacy! Think of the added impact our teaching would have on our children if they were to witness more consistency between what we say and what we do.

Children are always watching. They learn just as much from our actions—or inaction—as they do from our words. Imagine if we were intentional about living out the fruit of the Spirit (Galatians 5:22–23) as much as possible in everyday life!

I will never forget that once at a family gathering, I noticed a friend of the family hanging back, not engaging very much. I felt bad for him, so I sat beside him and struck up a conversation. We had a wonderful time, and at the end of the party, my daughter thanked me for what I had done. I didn't think anyone had noticed, but my daughter noticed. She was watching, and my actions had an effect on her.

Finally, my wife and I are generous with our time, talent, and treasure, pouring them out onto our daughters. This is a living reminder of legacy, and though my girls didn't always appreciate all of the hours and dollars spent supporting them in sports, music, after-school activities, and more, they eventually recognized the impact. It got them thinking about how they could use their time, talent, and treasure to impact others.

3. How can you nurture your family's individual strengths when handling wealth and responsibility? There is a good chance that even if you live a life of radical generosity, you will have assets that will need to be passed along to someone after you die—property, money, investments. If radical generosity is the goal, then the question of how much inheritance should be left to your direct descendants can be a difficult one. Rest assured that there are no right or wrong answers. The most important thing is that you are intentionally setting up your family to continue the Legacy Continuum going forward.

I've read that David Green, the owner of Hobby Lobby, a company with sales of $5.5 billion, has placed the entire company in a trust that doesn't allow any of his children or grandchildren to tap its coffers. Even he can't touch it! What's even more incredible is that all of his children and grandchildren willingly agreed and voluntarily signed a family mission and vision statement to this effect. Why? Because David Green prepared his team for a mission much greater than making more money. He is extending their family Legacy Continuum for many generations to come.

After much prayer and discussion, my wife and I determined that we would earmark the bulk of our estate for Kingdom work and our children would receive a minor share. This decision resulted from countless discussions with my wife and lots of prayer. I also sought the counsel of Christian financial advisors to maximize the amount that we would leave for Kingdom work. This was a fully thought-out decision that came from me *and* my wife by God's leading.

Our decision was not based on any concerns over our daughters' ability to handle their inheritance (though that is something that all parents should consider). Rather, it was based on our belief that all we have belongs to God. He has blessed us to be a blessing. God allowed us to see the long game of building and sustaining a Legacy Continuum that He can use for greater Kingdom work for generations to come.

I believe that it's important to focus on what your children need rather than what they may want. Sure, they'll *want* your million-dollar estate, but do they *need* it? Will it generate more generosity within them, or will they spend or hoard it for their own pleasure?

Children who understand the importance of legacy will also understand this thought process. When we informed our daughters of our decision, they didn't throw tantrums or engage in passive-aggressive ways of showing us that they were angry about it. Instead, they made it clear that they were fully on board with this decision. Vanessa completely understood and agreed with it right away, and Vivian even expressed relief. She had been unsure as to how she would handle a healthy inheritance, so this took the pressure off her. Both daughters are ready and willing to manage our legacy after we are gone, using a vast majority of our estate for Kingdom work. For some families, this journey will be more difficult.

In the Old Testament, we read about the importance of the birthright of the firstborn. The interesting thing is that if we follow the blessing of Abraham being passed down, we see a consistent pattern of the firstborn being rejected and a younger child receiving the blessing instead. I think of Ishmael and Isaac, Esau and Jacob, Reuben and Joseph. In each case, this firstborn blessing was given to someone who was undeserving of receiving it. In this, I believe that God shows us that His blessing comes by grace, not by merit.

This approach flies in the face of traditional thinking. Many children have come to expect an inheritance from their parents, and to take such a thing away will be no easy task! If your children are on board with the Legacy Continuum, then they should understand. But what if your children are not on board? What if you have a fractured family, with some who believe in and understand the Legacy Continuum and others who push against it?

First and foremost, pray. This decision is a personal one, and you need God's guidance to navigate it. Second, it's important to tell your children about your decision. Don't wait for them to find out after you've passed away; that would only confuse and enrage them. Instead, sit them down and make your case as to why you're giving most of your money to Kingdom work.

If they are believers, they should know that God owns it all to begin with. You're merely returning to Him that which was His from the start. If they don't know God, then you will have a much more difficult path. Still, your children need to respect your decision based on your beliefs. If they don't, then you shouldn't necessarily do anything to appease them. For your children, this may be a hard pill to swallow. But how you distribute your assets primarily relates to your obedience to God. While there may not be any easy solution, there is always the rewarding experience of seeking God's direction and the advice of others.

It is important to utilize the resources available to us when forming a team and training them for legacy. We don't have to do this alone or without guidance. Below is a list of what has helped to inform my thinking:

- National Christian Foundation[20]
- Generous Giving[21]
- Ron Blue Institute[22]
- Ron Blue Trust [23]
- Prayer
- Consultation with friends and experts
- Trial and error

It is immensely important to get your team fully on board with radical generosity. When everyone is part of the team, striving toward the same goal, this baton is passed much more seamlessly.

YOU CAN BE A VOICE IN SOMEONE'S LIFE DECADES FROM NOW

It's easy to think of our individual impact as being limited to the here and now. Hopefully, as you've started this journey, you've realized that your impact can be much greater than that. You are part of a relay team, and the baton is your legacy. It is passed from one person to the next, generation to generation, creating a Legacy Continuum that can go on indefinitely.

This legacy is so much more than a set of standards or values. This is your chance to be a voice in someone's life now and years from now. Think of it! You have the opportunity to speak change into your children and family members. Chances are that you will never know the full impact your legacy will have on future generations. It may lead to one of your descendants discovering a life purpose. For another, it could provide encouragement in a time of seeking. It may inspire people several generations after you to live influential lives of faith. The impacts are boundless, and the effects will reach far beyond what you can begin to conceive in your imagination.

Future generations will benefit from your work today when they receive the baton that you intentionally and strategically passed along to those who came after you. You don't even have to meet! Your descendants will be impacted by you because of your legacy-minded efforts today. If that isn't reason enough to start forming and training your team, then I don't know what is!

Chapter Five Notes

Preparing Your Team

Fellow citizens, why do you burn and scrape every stone to gather wealth and take so little care of your children to whom you must one day relinquish all?[24]

—Socrates

There is a difference between the head and the heart.

My head is very rational and practical. It helps me to take a reasoned approach to money. It helps me to discern which charities or philanthropic causes we should support, and it also guides much of my estate planning. It shows me what is most practical when it comes to dividing up my tangible wealth.

But running in tangent with this is my heart. This aspect of me is more pliable and emotional. It's the part of me that allows the Spirit to prompt me in the moment, helping me to be more generous with my children and with those I see are in need.

The rational side of me (my head) helps me to be effective.

The emotional side (my heart) helps me to give freely and without restraint. Many times, these two sides are at odds, but I have found that both, working together, are necessary for an effective Legacy Continuum.

TAKE THE LEAD

As we explored in Chapter One, I believe the truth that personal involvement plus insight plus money brings about lasting and effective Kingdom impact. I've seen it work. I've seen it transform legacy in a good way. The core of this concept is understanding that writing a check to someone in need is the easiest thing you can do. The hard part is actually getting involved with those in need so you can better understand what their needs are and the most effective way to address those needs, what to pray for, and how to overcome challenges along the way.

Getting a sense of the heartbeat of a cause and then jumping in with both feet is one of the hardest things you can do, yet it's the most effective approach for legacy building. Doing this requires both the head and the heart. It also requires your children and your children's children to pick up the baton after you're gone. But how do you teach this balance of the head and the heart?

It starts at the top. The leaders of a family must be on the same page. This may not be easy, especially if one is a believer and the other is not, but it is essential to moving forward and making the maximum impact possible.

Occasionally, I come across a family leader who takes a

cavalier approach to legacy planning. Such a leader is not effective! A lack of planning and clarity is almost as damaging as bad planning. King David taught us this. When he was nearing death, two of his sons, Adonijah and Solomon, were vying for his throne (1 Kings 1). This was happening even though God had already instructed David that Solomon would succeed him as king.

I can't help but think that if David had been more proactive in making his wishes known, all the drama that ensued could have been avoided. Adonijah amassed a following and, if it hadn't been for the prophet Nathan and Bathsheba's quick response, would have claimed the throne!

The surest way to cause division within a family is to be vague about inheritance and legacy. This is why family leaders and their families need to be on the same page.

I am amazed that some spouses don't communicate their desires to one another. They often don't talk about how they want to support their grandchildren financially or how they want their estate divided. They don't talk about their last wishes or whether they want to be buried or cremated. All of this lack of transparency seems to be getting worse.

The Wall Street Journal reported that young people were having to deal with the sudden deaths of their parents due to COVID-19.[25] They were completely unprepared. No one had taken the time to go over last wishes and estate plans, because everyone assumed that they had time. They thought that they could do it later.

Not only do leaders need to be clear and transparent, but they also need to engage family members intentionally in these discussions, even the difficult ones. Involving team members is a great way to help everyone grow in the head and the heart. While each member of the team functions within his or her role, you, as the leader, will be able to provide guidance, input, and direction. To do this, you must play to the passions of your family members.

PASSION AND PURPOSE

During our regularly scheduled Family Partnership Meetings (more on this later), we often consider new nonprofits and charitable organizations to support. This was jump-started because I wanted to give our daughters a more active role in determining how we give as a family. I invited them to propose charity options that they were excited about, that sparked something within them. Their reports included details of the organizations and why those causes were important to them.

For example, one area of interest for Vivian relates to human trafficking and sexual exploitation. When she and her family lived in Germany, she discovered that 150,000 people in Germany were living in forced prostitution and sexual exploitation. There's one particular ministry there she is exploring that is trying to reach women and give them the opportunity for a new beginning.

Also, when all brothels in Germany were closed due to COVID-19, many of the women in prostitution were without income and were living in poverty, another area of focus for this ministry. We can't wait to see how Vivian will involve herself in this!

Vanessa lives in Long Island City, New York, and she came to us during one of our Family Partnership Meetings, wanting us to support the City Harvest food bank there. She has a passion for New Yorkers who are in poverty, and her research showed how effective that organization was in meeting those needs.

I asked her for a full analysis. What kind of organization was this? How long had they been around? How did they use their funds? What impact were they having?

She came to us with a glowing report, showing that the organization wasn't just about providing food to the needy, but also about rescuing food from local farmers and restaurants so that it wouldn't be thrown away. In addition, the organization proved to be culturally and ethnically sensitive. They provided Hispanic food, Asian food—whatever was needed for the communities they served.

Vanessa's next step was to get more deeply involved with City Harvest. Offering them her time and talent would allow her to develop her knowledge of the organization. (She already had the heart in place!) She now serves on their junior board, and the relationships that she's developed have allowed her to propose a program to the organization that has a tighter connection to the Asian community in Chinatown, Manhattan.

Vanessa is a very busy professional. It would be easy for her to brush this off, saying that she doesn't have time. But she is invested in this process because it's important to her, *not* because I told her to find a mission.

If I had simply offered to write a check to her favorite charity, she wouldn't have had a chance to become emotionally and mentally invested in the process. She wouldn't have had an opportunity to help the organization focus on the struggles of the Asian community.

Society tends to think of Asian Americans as a model minority. There is the assumption that we work hard, and because we work hard, we don't have need. But that is not the case! Vanessa is opening people's eyes to this reality, all because she is investing time, talent, and treasure in this organization. She is nurturing generosity in her head and her heart for the maximum impact possible.

Here's the beauty of legacy. Through Vanessa's work, our entire family has experienced a heart change. We had no idea what some people were going through, and it's because of Vanessa that our eyes have been opened and our hearts have been softened. We're anticipating more of the same with whatever cause Vivian chooses.

It can be difficult to talk about money with your children, but it becomes a lot simpler if you reframe the conversation and talk about generosity goals instead. You might have millions of dollars in your account, and you might suspect that the moment you become transparent with your children, they'll start thinking about the Lamborghinis and vacation homes they'll buy. This is why many shy away from talking about money.

But if you reframe it so that you're talking about goals, then things change. When you focus on generosity, the money part becomes secondary. When your children and heirs are first and foremost invested in the family legacy and they see it being lived out from the top down, then their heads and their hearts will be impacted. They will begin to see the world through a Kingdom lens.

NEVER PASS ALONG WEALTH WITHOUT WISDOM

Offering up time and talent to worthy organizations is a good thing, but it's when you pair those efforts with treasure that you'll find your legacy beginning to multiply. I love the advice given in Ecclesiastes 7:11–12, which reads, "Wisdom is as good as an inheritance, yes, more excellent it is for those [the living] who see the sun. For wisdom is a defense even as money is a defense, but the excellency of knowledge is that wisdom shields and preserves the life of him who has it" (AMPC). The following explanation of these verses aligns with my understanding of this passage:[26]

These verses briefly examine one of the properties that wisdom and money share. The key word is "share." Notice that the term "better" does not appear in the context. The reason is that wisdom is so superior to wealth that it derives no additional glory from it. If a person has both, that is of course good. However, if they are personified, one must conclude that wisdom could do better without wealth than wealth could do without wisdom.

The attribute that they share is the power to protect, to be a defense or a shade, as some translations say, against life's difficulties. Even in regard to this quality, the comparison reveals that wisdom is of greater value. The comparison

> shows that wisdom is like a wall of protection whereas wealth is merely a hedge. In adversity, wisdom provides reserves of strength to the person who possesses it. Wealth, though, continues to feed a person's self-importance and lusts, and so it may even be detrimental to progress.

It's almost taboo to talk about money or tangible wealth in Christian circles. There is an assumption that talking about money equals a love of money, so people shy away from the topic. But money can be a powerful force for good in the world! First Timothy 6:18 reads, "Tell them to use their money to do good" (NLT). After all, doesn't money come from God?

I encourage you to shift your thinking when it comes to money and tangible wealth. Instead of viewing it as the root of all evil or as something to be hoarded or used to satisfy your selfish wants, recognize that it's a powerful tool to benefit other people and grow your legacy.

All of this starts with passing along a love for the Lord as outlined in Deuteronomy 6:5–9. The next step is to raise your family with godly values and a strong work ethic. Even if you never achieve a high net worth, there is a good chance that your children will.

Consider that most millionaires are self-made. They come from lower- or middle-class beginnings. Also consider that most millionaires don't have high-paying jobs. Self-made millionaires can be teachers, tradespeople, and blue-collar workers.

Even if you never achieve millionaire status, at some point

in your life, you will have to make decisions about tangible wealth. What's more is that the wealth that God gives you can be used to shape your wisdom and legacy.

The consequences of passing on wealth without first endeavoring to impart knowledge and wisdom can be disastrous. Not only will the wealth be wasted, but it may also damage future generations.

How do you ensure that you gain knowledge and wisdom to handle your tangible wealth? There are some truths I live by. First, we shouldn't be transferring tangible wealth to adult children unless we've first imparted wisdom to them. That wisdom will teach them what money is and what it isn't and how to seek God's direction for its use.

Second, it's important to gain additional knowledge and wisdom from a variety of sources. There are three categories of people from whom I glean financial intelligence:

- *Financial advisors*—these are wealth planners, tax advisors, and so on.

- *Family, friends, and even strangers*—I love asking people about their perspectives on wealth! I weigh what they say, and if I find a nugget of wisdom, then I'll implement that in my approach. Some of the best financial advice I've received has come from strangers.

- *Expert resources*—this includes organizations and "celebrities" in the field, such as the National Christian Foundation, Dave Ramsey, and Ron Blue.

I have learned so much by reading their books and

researching their methods.

Third, it's important to have a Christian estate attorney. Working with someone like this will enable you early on to tackle tough questions, such as:

- How much should you leave your children? Does it make sense to divide your estate equally among your children?

- Should you begin advancing your children's inheritance before you die? If so, when will you start? How much will you start with?

- What part of your estate will go to Kingdom work?

Allow me to offer a final word on working with financial experts. Of course, you can receive excellent financial advice from experts regardless of their faith and beliefs. However, my personal experience is that working with Christian professionals facilitates the collaborative experience: shared faith makes tackling the tough questions easier. This is why I strongly encourage choosing Christian financial experts. They will tend to understand more readily and fully where you're coming from—and, accordingly, provide insight and ideas in line with your legacy mission.

The best way to find a Christian estate attorney is by asking other Christians (family, friends, business acquaintances, church people, etc.). If you are already working with a Christian accountant or Christian financial advisor, you could consider asking him or her for recommendations.

ACHIEVE FINANCIAL LITERACY

My wife and I made many financial sacrifices over the years to stay out of debt. We denied ourselves vacations and luxury cars. If we took our daughters to the movie theater, it was to the one-dollar theater showing second- or third-run films. We didn't lavish them with more toys than they needed, either. Much of this came from the legacy I inherited from my parents. The way that they saved and managed money stuck with me, and thankfully, my wife was on the same page.

I believe that God blessed us as a result of the way we viewed and handled money. We were financially literate early on, and it has resulted in God entrusting more wealth to us later in life. I think of Luke 16:10: "Whoever can be trusted with very little can also be trusted with much" (NIV).

Financial literacy is all about knowing how to put money to work for you. It's about living below your means. It's about understanding the power of financial investments and choosing to invest rather than to spend. I heard a nugget of wisdom many years ago: "It's not about how much you make, but how much you save."[27] That message has remained with me and impacts my spending habits to this day.

For many, this kind of living is unappealing because it requires sacrifice and discipline. After all, it's not always easy to forego that Disney vacation in exchange for maxing out your IRA that year. But without financial literacy, you will never grow tangible wealth.

Think of it this way: financial literacy is about doing things today that will help your family to improve financially for generations to come. It's about demonstrating a prudent way of living, and it involves educating your family on how to spend money, how to save it, and how to give it away. I'm not talking about living without. I'm talking about knowing when and how to spend money.

One of the most effective ways that I've found to talk with my family about financial literacy is to explore the mistakes people tend to make with money. Many people do not live within their means. They live on credit, and those payments pile up. Many people fail to save for emergencies, and they also fail to invest for the long term. Many people live without a budget, spending each paycheck when they receive it. Using these real-world examples can have quite the impact!

Another aspect of financial literacy is knowing about estate planning. Explain to your family what a will is and why and when they need one. Talk about what living trusts are and why they're important. Furthermore, don't just tell them about all the sound financial decisions you've made; also tell them about the financial blunders. By exposing them to this knowledge early on, you will get them thinking about the importance of establishing these tools in their own lives.

As parents, we have the opportunity and privilege to impact the future with the values and wisdom we feel strongly about. My parents were uneducated people. They, especially my mom, never had the opportunity to pursue an education in China. Even after my dad immigrated to the U. S., his English language skills were minimal. However, that did not deter my parents from doing all they could to support and encourage my siblings and me in our educational pursuits.

Let's build on the work our parents did and provide our families with the knowledge of not only the importance of education, but also how to begin preparing financially for it. You can do this by exploring how you can collaborate to fund the educational needs of future generations.

God has blessed my wife and me, so I want to be a blessing to my daughters and grandchildren by providing financial support for higher education. College funds take financial pressure off my daughters and their spouses, and they set my grandchildren up for success. They also highlight the importance of higher education, which is something that is key to our family's Legacy Continuum. It's important that my grandchildren and great-grandchildren be well educated.

There are many ways to provide future educational funds. The one I like is the 529 Plan, as it is more efficient than giving cash. Of course, there are some considerations. We want to be sensitive here, particularly to sons-in-law or daughters-in-law who may not want any financial assistance for their children's college education. They may feel that the financial responsibility should be theirs alone. In other words, don't surprise them with a 529. Talk about it first and be considerate of their desires. If they want to provide the funds for their children's education, then you can find another way to set your grandchildren up for success.

Also, don't feel as though you have to do all or nothing. You may not be financially able to contribute as much as you'd like, but I am here to tell you that any amount, no matter how small, is better than no amount. The goal here is to encourage education and help our grandchildren (and beyond) to get started in life. Secondarily, it takes some of the financial burden off our children. As a result, everyone will be more equipped to continue the family legacy.

TEACH AND LIVE OUT GENEROSITY

In his book *The Treasure Principle*, Randy Alcorn states, "Giving is the only antidote to materialism."[28] It's a powerful reminder that the more you give, the less attached to this world you will become. I strive to ensure that my family understands and lives this principle. Perhaps the best example of this is in how we are handling inheritance.

After much prayer and plenty of lengthy—sometimes uncomfortable—discussions with our daughters, we've decided as a family on the following plan:

- Most of my and Elina's estate will go to Kingdom work.

- Our children have the responsibility of stewarding the money we've put aside, the bulk of our estate, that will be designated for Kingdom work. In other words, much of these funds would have added to their inheritance. They not only understand that, but are also totally on board with it and are glad to do it, per the decisions we've made as a family.

- They will then use some of those funds to prepare the next generation to extend the family legacy, thus triggering the Legacy Continuum.

- They will pass on our family's faith, values, beliefs, and wisdom *before* a single penny is dispersed.

- They will continue to grow the family giving fund with their own efforts after we are gone.

The driving force behind all of this is for us to continue to learn and demonstrate generosity. Without that, we have nothing. Without that, all of these efforts are in vain.

The Treasure Principle also states that "God gives us more money than we need so we can give—generously."[29] I couldn't agree more. The key is not only to believe this, but also to live it. The more you teach, encourage, and demonstrate generosity, the more your family will learn to be generous. And the smarter you are about it, combining your head and your heart, the more effective it all will be.

There are unlimited ways you can start small and practice generosity with your family now, such as:

- Bring food or snacks to a nursing home and spend time interacting with the people there. (The elderly enjoy having children around!)

- Respond to a natural disaster by giving needed items. Have your children take the lead in choosing the items you donate and perhaps have them pay for it out of their allowance.

- Spend time cleaning up a neighbor's yard or joining a church's community support initiatives.

- Have your children volunteer to mow the lawn of an elderly couple.

- Volunteer as a family at a local nonprofit.

- Read a book about generosity together and discuss what it means to them individually as well as for the family.

Ecclesiastes 2:18–21 (NET) has a thought-provoking take on wealth and inheritance:

> So I loathed all the fruit of my effort, for which I worked so hard on earth, because I must leave it behind in the hands of my successor. Who knows if he will be a wise man or a fool? Yet he will be master over all the fruit of my labor for which I worked so wisely on earth. This also is futile! So I began to despair about all the fruit of my labor for which I worked so hard on earth. For a man may do his work with wisdom, knowledge, and skill; however, he must hand over the fruit of his labor as an inheritance to someone else who did not work for it.

The truth is that we can never guarantee that our successors will handle our tangible and intangible wealth wisely. But the more you prepare your family and introduce them to generosity, the greater the chance that they will embrace the Legacy Continuum in their own lives. '

Opportunities to show generosity are endless, and each one will bring you closer to your goal of having a solid team focused on your family's legacy. As you grow as a family and as individuals, learning to utilize the head and the heart effectively, you will naturally progress to bigger goals and better objectives.

NARROW THE CONVERSATION

Some time ago, I was listening to a podcast in which the speaker was talking about the stages of a conversation. He said that the natural flow of discussion has phases of converging and diverging.

When you diverge, you expand the conversation. You touch on different things, new ideas, and unique topics. The things you discuss may not even tie together, but that's okay. That's the art of conversation.

But there comes a point—or multiple points—in every conversation where you have to converge. When you converge, you narrow the conversation. You find the thing that you can focus on for a while. Then, if you continue the conversation, eventually you'll have to diverge again, and the cycle repeats itself.

All that you have read up to this point may seem like the diverging of topics. We've touched on many different ideas and truths. We've talked about preparing your heart and the importance of legacy. We've talked about intangible wealth and how your story impacts who you are. We've talked about taking your legacy mission and bringing it to your family, expanding it to become a relay race instead of a solo sprint. We've talked about identifying the strengths and purpose of your individual family members and learning to work as a team to have maximum impact for generations to come. And we've talked about making generosity a combined effort of the head and the heart.

The next chapter will bring everything together. It will be the point of convergence for everything we've discussed so far. Your team will find alignment and your legacy will begin to take shape as you approach the race prepared, equipped, and energized.

Chapter Six Notes

A Family Mission Statement

But from everlasting to everlasting the LORD's love is with those who fear him, and his righteousness with their children's children—with those who keep his covenant and remember to obey his precepts.

—Psalm 103:17–18 *(NIV)*

It takes work and training to learn how to run with and pass a baton, but there's something much bigger going on in a relay race. The runners on a team may have different strengths and individual roles to play, but they are all focused on a single goal: to finish strong and win.

Winning doesn't come by chance. You have to cross the finish line first, which means that you have to outpace your opponents, pass the baton swiftly, and have the necessary endurance and speed. If each person on the team were to perform his or her task without the overarching goal of winning in mind, the race would look a lot different! Runners might not stay in their lanes. They might not even make it around the track, let alone cross the finish line. A clear, single goal that requires each person's individual performance is crucial to running and finishing a relay race well.

The same is true of the Legacy Continuum. Without a clear focus, without a framework for what you are doing and where you are going, you risk a poorly run race. Of course, God can take a poorly run race and still use it for His glory, but He has given us everything we need to succeed. Why would you spend a lifetime building this up if you aren't going to do everything in your power to ensure that you finish strong?

This is where the family mission statement comes into play. Just like the personal mission statement that helps to frame your goals and work here on earth, the family mission statement provides a framework for your team to run the race. It's a crucial element to make sure that you and your family run and finish strong.

FAMILY MISSION STATEMENTS
BRING STABILITY

When I was growing up, my family was not perfect—no family is—but I had a great sense of stability. Our family structure was very traditional, with a mother and father and three children. My parents were married for nearly seventy years, and while my father was strict, he certainly wasn't abusive. My parents were present in my life and wanted me to succeed. This stability helped me to feel secure, despite the many trials my parents faced as immigrants struggling to make ends meet. My family was my constant, offering a sense of protection and security.

Unfortunately, not every child has this blessing. Family instability is the new norm.[30] A Pew Research Center Study of 130 countries and territories showed that the U. S. has the world's highest rate of children living in single-parent households.[31] Princeton University sociologist Sara McLanahan has noted, "If we were asked to design a system for making sure that children's basic needs were met, we would probably come up with something quite similar to the two-parent family ideal."[32]

Families are broken and hurting, and yours may be one of them. What more incentive do you need to reset the race and establish who you are and what kind of legacy you will leave? One way of accomplishing this is to have honest, difficult discussions that work toward the development of a family mission statement.

The family mission statement provides guidance and identity. Stephen Covey wrote, "A family mission statement is a combined, unified expression from all family members of what your family is all about—what it is you really want to do and be—and the principles you choose to govern your family life."[33]

From this quote, I came up with three questions a family can ask to help craft a family mission statement:

1. What kind of a family do we want to be?

2. What does our family want to accomplish together?

3. What values and principles will guide the actions of our family?

Answering these questions will help to stabilize your Legacy Continuum and focus your family efforts.

FAMILY MISSION STATEMENTS REINFORCE FAITH

When your family begins to think about what you all want to be and do and where you want to go and you come together for a unified purpose, you'll find that it brings more than stability; it will also help to reinforce your faith. I believe that God created the family unit. In the beginning, when God created man, He said, "It is not good for the man to be alone" (Genesis 2:18 NIV). So God created woman (Genesis 2:18–24) and then blessed the man and woman and told them to have children (Genesis 1:28).

God loves the family unit and wants it to glorify Him. To understand how to glorify God as a family, we can draw from the Apostle Paul's epistle to the church in Colossae. He wrote a beautiful passage that I believe can be a starting point for discussing the type of family you want to be:

Therefore, as God's chosen people, holy and dearly loved, clothe yourselves with compassion, kindness, humility,

gentleness and patience. Bear with each other and forgive one another if any of you has a grievance against someone. Forgive as the Lord forgave you. And over all these virtues put on love, which binds them all together in perfect unity.
—Colossians 3:12–14 *(NIV)*

In Galatians 5, Paul also listed nine specific qualities that believers should develop and demonstrate: "love, joy, peace, forbearance, kindness, goodness, faithfulness, gentleness and self-control" (Galatians 5:22–23 NIV). These characteristics are the result of the work of the Holy Spirit in a Christian's life. A family that exudes these traits shows that the Spirit is at work in the entire family!

DEVELOP A FAMILY MISSION STATEMENT

If a family needs stability and a shared mission statement helps them to achieve that while also helping them to grow in their faith, then what is there to lose? Your relay race can be much more effective if you and your family take the steps of putting pen to paper and coming up with your overarching family goal.

There are plenty of online resources that will help you through the process of developing a family mission statement. The important thing is that you do whatever works best for your family. Perhaps a workbook would be helpful or a Bible study based on the fruit of the Spirit. You might make great progress using the list of three questions I posed earlier in the chapter. Perhaps you could watch an

121

inspiring video to kick-start your brainstorming session. Bringing in a third-party mediator, such as a pastor or advisor, may also be a great way to facilitate discussion.

Each family has a unique chemistry, and the more you cater to that, the more effective you will be. This comes back to knowing your family members well—their strengths, shortcomings, and mindsets. The better you know them, the more likely you are to find an approach that works well.

One of the most important guidelines, however, is to start slow. Try not to rush the process. You may become frustrated and feel that you're not making the progress you had hoped for, but *the process is more important than the actual product.*

It may be tempting to try to turn this into a business meeting. It may be tempting to try to incorporate SMART goals and corporate jargon, but this is about family. It's about making little Sally feel just as involved and excited as you are. It's about inclusion and welcoming thoughts and ideas. It's a conversation more than it is a board meeting.

My family began the process by searching Scripture for a verse that would capture the heart of our family. It took some time, but God led us to Luke 3:11, which reads, "Whoever has two tunics is to share with him who has none, and whoever has food is to do likewise" (ESV). The concept of "two tunics" has become our family banner statement and the reason behind our actions.

Then we went to work compiling our hopes, dreams, and desires. We prayed on them and eventually were able to bring them all together in a mission statement. Just like my personal mission statement, the family mission statement changes from time to time. This is how it currently reads:

> Two Tunics Legacy is an expression of God's abounding generosity. Our mission is to live out and promote the call to action in Luke 3:11. We do this by engaging, challenging, and partnering with others to visibly demonstrate the power of God's provision and compassion to a world in need.

This statement guides the entire family, keeping us on course and in the race to a Legacy Continuum. It's almost become part of our DNA. It motivates how we think and talk. It guides, corrects, and encourages us. It gives us a strong sense of identity and togetherness and allows us to fight for generosity as a unit. "Two tunics" has become like a code phrase for our family. When we refer to it, everyone in our family knows that a serious discussion will take place regarding our mission as a family to be insanely generous stewards of our blessings from God. When we identify a need in the world, we know where to take that need.

YOUR FAMILY'S COMPASS FOR GENERATIONS

My family and I came together and created this mission statement, and now we use it to guide our actions. It's our North Star, always constant, yet it changes here and there to ensure that our efforts are the best they can be. Let me give you an example.

For the better part of a decade, our family's approach to giving was very traditional. We picked a handful of organizations that we would support with our time, talent, and finances, and we divided our giving accordingly.

Then COVID-19 hit, and we had to rethink what we were doing and why. Political and cultural tensions, paired with the pandemic, had created a chasm of need. We wanted to regroup, to take a step back. We knew that we needed to rethink how our small family fund could impact the world to help renew and restore it in this time of great need. We decided that it was time to lean into our mission statement and discover what it really means to "demonstrate the power of God's provision and compassion to a world in need."

During this time, Vanessa drew our attention to many communities in the Middle East. A revival is occurring there. People are having dreams about God, and it's causing them to abandon Islam for Christianity. This idea that God was using dreams really connected with our family. The more we explored it, the more we felt compelled to support people's dreams. We ultimately did this through a joint program called The Dream Forum by the nonprofit Goldenwood (more on this in Chapter Ten). This organization states the following about dreams:[34]

> We take seriously the reality that we have a God who speaks to us, and who gives us dreams of His Kingdom so that we might cultivate this world in ways that reflect His character and embody His glory. ... [O]ur hope is to encourage listening—listening to the Spirit of God, in community, as He invites us to take up the calling we've received—a calling to reimagine and remake our world with love.

Working with Goldenwood, we have sponsored individuals who have incredible dreams for the future. These people use their skills and abilities to reach the homeless, help foster kids, and so much more. We're able to offer financial backing to people who have dreams that can truly change lives! Partnering with them has been such a blessing, and it wouldn't have happened if we hadn't opened ourselves up and asked God what plans He had for our mission statement.

These are the results that a unified, loving, bold family mission statement can generate in the world. Imagine what can happen if a mission is passed from generation to generation! The impact for the Kingdom is infinite, and the connection that your family will have from generation to generation can be life-giving.

In a relay race, the baton is the only thing that is constant. Every runner touches it. Moreover, the baton needs to be carried for the duration of the race, or the team is disqualified. Your mission statement is encapsulated in your baton. It will remain with your family from generation to generation. Different personalities will carry it. Different runners will do their part. But the mission statement will remain. This is why establishing a mission statement is so critical to the success of the Legacy Continuum.

THE REWARD IS WORTH THE JOURNEY

Veteran runners in a relay race can make passing the baton

look so effortless, so smooth. They don't make mistakes. They work together as a true team should, never wavering or faltering. Many of us will never know how hard these athletes work to achieve this level of success on the track.

Reality, however, is much different. Those runners trained for years to be able to do what they do so well. They overcame setbacks, disadvantages, injuries, and poor dynamics. They pushed through when it got tough and put in the time and effort needed to be great at what they do.

The same is true for your family. The first time you pick up the baton will have its share of difficulty and setbacks. There will be opinions to weigh and family dynamics that you'll have to work through. It's a long-term process that will take time and patience, but it's also a great opportunity to learn from each other, laugh, have fun, and maybe even cry together.

In the same way that runners understand the process of training to become great, you also need to understand that you're not going to get it right on day one or even day one hundred. The important thing is that you keep learning, keep growing, and keep talking.

There will be times when you think that you've hit a breakthrough, only for the team to revert back to old habits. There will be times when you're the only person talking. There will be commitment issues and inconsistencies. There will be an aversion to vulnerability. All of this is part of the process, and if you stick with it, you will one day be a smooth-running team.

Remember that this is completely new for you. You're

going down a trail that doesn't have markers or even a clear path. It's going to be difficult; it's going to be bumpy. But if you pay attention and keep moving step after step, with God's help, you will make progress.

The end result will be a family mission statement that will be your baton for generations to come. It will be a road map for how to treat one another, how to handle family conflict, how to forgive one another. It will be a blueprint for how to change the world.

Your family mission statement will be a message of love to one another and then to the world. When that message becomes part of your family, that's when you'll start to see your legacy multiply.

Chapter Seven Notes

_____

_____

_____

_____

_____

_____

_____

_____

_____

_____

_____

_____

_____

_____

_____

_____

_____

_____

_____

_____

PART THREE: GO!

Your Role as a Coach

And let us consider how to stir up one another to love and good works, not neglecting to meet together, as is the habit of some, but encouraging one another, and all the more as you see the Day drawing near.

—Hebrews 10:24–25 *(ESV)*

In "On Your Mark," you soul-searched to find what was really important and developed a personal mission statement. In "Get Set," you brought your family on board and leveraged their individual strengths to unleash the multiplier effect as described in Chapter One. You also developed a family mission statement and began the important new habit of meeting together to discuss your family's Legacy Continuum. You have taken your *mark*, you are *set*, and now it's time to *GO!*

In a relay race, the command to *GO* is when everything comes together. Months, perhaps years, of training and careful strategizing culminate in a great show of ability.

Runners perform with everything they have, each doing his or her part for the greater goal. But the runners are not alone. They have each other.

GO is about doing generosity as a family. It's about leveraging your collective time, talent, and treasure for the benefit of God's kingdom. It's about meeting together regularly to share dreams, goals, ideas, successes, and struggles. To be successful in this, you'll need to provide great leadership and a finish-line mindset.

At my high school track meets, just before I approached the starting line, my coach would give me a brief pep talk and last-minute instructions. He'd remind me to stay low at the start, or he'd tell me to imagine that I was running on hot coals (I always loved that one). He was instrumental on race day, just as he was in all of the practices leading up to it.

This chapter is about your role as a coach in the *GO* phase. It offers some ideas and practices that have worked for me over the years. While it's impossible for you to anticipate everything, you can be mentally prepared for the race ahead. Your team will look to you for instruction and direction, and they will draw their strength and confidence from you as well.

This race doesn't need to be perfect. It doesn't need to be fast. It just needs to move you toward the goal.

Visualize Your *GO*

When good runners visualize a race before running it, they imagine every stride, every movement, before their feet ever hit the track. Similarly, before your family "goes," you must have a plan.

Your family will be looking to you to guide them through the process of *GO* as they help to carry forward what God has given. They may ask:

- Why is this important?

- What do you want me to do?

- How do we move forward?

It's important to anticipate these kinds of questions, and it's also important to anticipate pushback. Your family may not fully agree with your answers or perspectives.

For example, one of your children may feel strongly about current social justice issues. He or she might propose that the family support such causes, only for another family member to disagree. Do you see how this could turn into a contentious issue? Perhaps even reading about it is giving you sweaty palms!

You may find yourself having to walk a tightrope. On one hand, you'll want to engage your family and accommodate their passions. On the other hand, you may have to set some basic guidelines.

For my family, we have agreed that we will support various causes that are close to the hearts of Asian Americans. Since the start of the COVID-19 pandemic in 2020, the level of anti-Asian racism and xenophobia expression has grown in this country. The media has reported a spike in incidents of anti-Asian harassment, verbal abuse, bullying, and violence, especially against older members of the Asian American community. This greatly saddens us.

However, many of the current needs of this movement are politically motivated, something that doesn't line up with our family mission statement, so we have to be careful. We have to approach it with discernment. Individual family members are free to donate to or support political causes personally, but when it comes to the family legacy, we try to stay away from choosing sides, so to speak.

Therefore, we chose another path for supporting Asian American communities during this difficult time. Through Vanessa's involvement with a food rescue charity in New York City, we discovered that there are some elderly Asian Americans who depend on food pantries for their sustenance. Unfortunately, these food pantries have limited supplies of Asian produce with which these people are familiar. This has become a target project for us to work on.

While I'm thankful that my family came to this agreement relatively easily, your family may push back more. Trying to get everyone on the same page will often take longer than you think, but in the end, the results will be that much more rewarding. This is why visualizing your family meetings and having a plan, a framework, is so crucial to success. You don't want something unexpected to throw you off course.

Pushback and disagreements can arise from healthy differences in perspective, personality, and God's leading of individual family members. My wife, Elina, has always had a passion for funding faith-driven causes, like missionaries or the global church. Her reasoning is sound. Funding for these causes will undoubtedly come from a smaller segment of the population than, say, funding for children in poverty. Therefore, Elina's giving tends to gravitate toward the intersection of faith and need. Each member of your team will have his or her own giving sweet-spot.

Yet, even if you share with your family what God has put on your heart, and even if you set boundaries and welcome discussion, you may run into a number of threats when family members disagree with your approach.

1. Resentment: We've discussed this in a previous chapter, but you may have a son or a daughter who feels as though you're giving away his or her inheritance. This can become a big problem within the family dynamics, threatening your group's ability to move forward.

2. Animosity: You may have a domineering family member who will push the family off course. When this happens, family members may disengage from the process or remain silent. This can destroy the team, and it's up to you to ensure that everyone feels included and that no single person dictates the group's direction.

Resentment and animosity are dangers, but there's an even greater threat.

3. Satan is intent on preventing you from accomplishing your mission. His goal is to cause you to drop the baton. As long as he can prevent the baton from being passed from one generation to another, then he will be effective at bringing an end to your legacy of faith, beliefs, history, experience, wisdom, and generosity.

In 2 Corinthians 10:3–4, we're reminded that our struggle isn't against people, but against the forces that are unseen. One of my favorite Christian leaders, J. D. Greear, says, "As long as we confess Jesus as Lord and have the Spirit of God within us, Satan will do everything he can to destroy our faith."[35]

Being aware that Satan wants to destroy what you're building is part of visualizing your *GO*. But you need to be more than aware. You need to be prepared.

We're in a spiritual battle, but we aren't defenseless. Ephesians 6:11 instructs us to "put on the full armor of God" (NIV) and to "stand firm against all strategies of the devil" (NLT).

Study Ephesians 6. Take it to heart. Claim the promises found there. That is the basis for how to visualize your *GO*.

KEEP YOUR EYES ON THE PATH AHEAD

In addition to visualizing the race and anticipating problems, my track coach wanted us to keep our eyes open. We needed to be aware of our surroundings. He'd instruct us to be on the lookout for possible dangers, such as loose debris, low-lying wet areas, and trip hazards. The more we anticipated those obstacles, the better and more confident we became at overcoming them.

When it comes to family legacy discussions, there are just as many pitfalls that you'll need to watch out for. You can't be certain that they will pop up, but you need to be ready nonetheless.

As you come together as a family to give shape to your legacy and put your family mission statement into action, you'll find that there will be many decisions that have to be made. Getting into the nuts and bolts of what and how to give and to whom to give it can be quite the process. The timing and the amount of time, talent, and treasure you give will depend on your family situation. The members of your team will be looking to you for leadership, guidance, and encouragement.

Each topic and decision could bring some unexpected obstacles, which is why you'll want to seek a consensus on key decisions as much as possible. Consensus will keep the team moving in a positive direction. As you grow as a team, you'll find ways in which your family best reaches a consensus.

One way that may work for you is to take a vote. Some time ago, I served on the governing board of a new church plant. One of the first decisions we made was that we would always seek a unanimous vote on critical issues. If you're familiar with boards and with business, this may sound nearly impossible! However, we felt strongly about achieving unity as a board.

With that in mind, we stepped out in faith that God would help us to attain that level of unity. If we came to a stalemate on a big issue, we'd table it. We'd go home, pray, and have a chance to reconsider our positions, plus the opinions of others. Later, we'd revisit the topic. If we still had a stalemate, we'd table it again. Occasionally, we tabled some issues several times before reaching a unanimous decision, but we always reached a decision in a reasonable time frame.

When it comes to minor issues, you will have to seek a compromise. For example, if your family finances are limited and one child wants to give $100 to one mission, but the other child wants to give $200 to a different mission, then there are many potential compromises. One option would be to give $150 to each mission. Another possibility would be to support one mission this year and the next mission next year. Whichever middle ground you pick, you'll have to understand the benefits and concessions for each party when coming to a final decision.

As a leader, you'll have to utilize wisdom, and it's going to take effort. It's going to take energy and thought. You'll have to strike a balance between maintaining control and welcoming input, ideas, and some healthy pushback.

When navigating these obstacles:

- Encourage the even-tempered, coolheaded, and reasonable family members to speak up and engage. These people tend to set a good tone for the meetings.

- Deal with conflict right away. Conflict has a way of creeping it. It may happen quickly and when you least expect it. The sooner the conflict is resolved, the better.

- Look to the peacemakers in the group to assist.

- Focus on the areas of agreement; don't dwell on the differences.

- Expect disagreements. If you need to table the issue or take a break, do so.

- Stay above the fray. When a heated argument erupts, don't add to the fracas. Be the peacemaker. Paul wrote, "Finally, brothers and sisters, whatever is true, whatever is noble, whatever is right, whatever is pure, whatever is lovely, whatever is admirable—if anything is excellent or praiseworthy—think about such things" (Philippians 4:8 NIV).

- Cut each other some slack and demonstrate grace. Ephesians 4:29 reads, "Let no corrupting talk come out of your mouths, but only such as is good for building up, as fits the occasion, that it may give grace to those who hear" (ESV).

At the end of the day, if all you have to give each other is grace, then you're heading in the right direction. Giving grace also gives freedom. Grace allows people to be themselves, to be who God created them to be. Grace doesn't criticize. Grace isn't defensive. Grace doesn't rush to make a point or try to win an argument.

Grace makes room for people to be open and honest, and it may be the only thing that holds your family meetings together at first. Staying focused and bringing grace into the discussion will help you to navigate your surroundings and run with confidence.

LEAD WITH GRACE

My many years in corporate America gave me a fun superpower. I can step into a meeting of strangers, and within five minutes, I can tell you who the leaders are.

The leaders are the ones to whom other people defer. They're the ones who are asked for their input. They may or may not be talkative. They may or may not be extroverts. They may poke fun at themselves and not take themselves too seriously. But everyone around them thinks of them as leaders, whether their job title denotes it or not.

Leadership isn't about standing up and saying, "I'm the leader!" People who have to do that aren't genuine leaders. Just because someone has authority, which would be reflected in a job title and on the company's organization chart, doesn't necessarily mean that he or she is a genuine leader.

If you're reading this book and you have every intention of moving your family through this process, then chances are that you're one of your family's leaders—and everyone in your family already knows it! For some, becoming an inspiring leader takes an enormous amount of effort. For others, effective leadership is almost effortless. Regardless of what type of leader you are at your core, when you step up with God in your heart and take the head role, it increases the chance that others will respond. It gives them confidence in the process. If your intentions, words, and actions are sincere, righteous, and focused on others rather than yourself, your family members will feel it and respect it.

We may assume that leaders have to be perfect, but that's not the case. Good leaders admit to their mistakes and don't take themselves too seriously. Good leaders ask for help!

Good leaders also recognize that the primary goal is to get the team excited and engaged. Once they've gotten the ball rolling, they know when it's time to get out of the way. To get that proverbial ball rolling (or re-rolling if it has slowed down), you'll need to be prepared. These family discussions will be so wide-ranging that focus will quickly become an issue. It will be up to you to bring the team back to center.

Here's a method that has worked with my family meetings.

1. I start the discussion by reviewing our current giving plan. Some great questions for the family to consider include:

- Are we satisfied with our tithe amount and how effectively is it being used?

- Should we give beyond our current tithe with additional offerings?

- Beyond our tithes and offerings, how are we giving our time and talent for the benefit of others?

- What is the Holy Spirit saying to us? Where is God directing us to give beyond our tithe?

Remember that the goal should be a more focused, intentional, and strategic way of giving your family's collective time, talent, and treasure.

This discussion topic has changed my family. There is

much controversy over the tithe, but I believe that Scripture is clear on what our attitude should be toward giving. Second Corinthians 9:7 reads, "Each one must give as he has decided in his heart, not reluctantly or under compulsion, for God loves a cheerful giver" (ESV).

I believe that many Christians misunderstand the concept of tithes and offerings. They often focus on the tithe as giving a tenth of their earnings to God, but the truth is that the tithe is simply returning a portion of what was already His to begin with! But why would we stop there? God's generosity is boundless, and we have all shared in that bounty in so many ways.

When it came to my family, our struggle wasn't whether or not to tithe. What we needed was a renewed heart toward God, a heart of generosity. I'll never forget when, shortly after my wife and I became Christians, we were invited to listen to a speaker who talked about trusting God with your finances. Afterwards, I remember sitting in the car with my wife, and we were shaken. It was clear to us that God wanted us to begin a journey of generosity, and it began with a commitment to tithe. Over time, the truth of 2 Corinthians 9:7 became more real to us. We saw God's provision as we trusted Him with what was His in the first place!

During a recent small-group discussion with long-time friends, we were talking about generosity. In that discussion, someone confessed that he had a hard time giving spontaneously to someone on the street, such as a stranger who might use it for drugs or alcohol.

Of course, none of us want our generosity to cause more

harm than good, but when we talked about it more, the real issue came out. His fear of being taken advantage of exceeded his desire to be generous.

As a group, we were able to show him that he could trust God with the nominal amounts that people on the street were asking him for. How they would choose to spend the money shouldn't be his concern; that was God's concern. However, with larger amounts, due diligence is required.

Through this discussion, my friend uncovered his barrier and was given tangible ways he could work through it. What a rich discussion this was for our group!

Talking about our current giving plan can pave the way for honest, meaningful, and life-changing conversations. When we discuss *why* we have approached giving the way we have, that's when we can begin to uncover the voices we're listening to. Vulnerability is key, and you, as the leader, can set that standard by being open and vulnerable.

2. I make sure that the conversation pushes discussion to the next level. To get yourself in the right mindset as the family leader, consider the following questions:

- To ignite our family giving, what are some of the best ways to set aside a certain amount of money for the family to give away?

- What goals do I want to achieve with my family with respect to the collective giving of our time, talent, and treasure?

- Should I consult with our financial advisor to understand the most tax-advantaged ways of making donations?

With your responses in mind, some great questions to ask your family are:

- Is God prompting us to increase our generosity?

- What will each of us sacrifice in order for us to give more generously?

- What other areas of need has God placed on our hearts that the family should consider? Why?

- What expenses can we eliminate?

It's easy to become content with a certain level of giving, but these family meetings are about pushing the boundaries of what's considered normal. A common belief is that a tithe should be 10 percent of income. Sadly, it turns out that many Christians do not tithe at all:[36]

> Setting aside the argument about whether God intends Christians to tithe or not, the number of people who give at least ten percent of their income to the church is less than a quarter.

Can you imagine what would happen if Christians all around the world were to begin giving away 90 percent of what they have? When reflecting on this, keep in mind Malachi 3:10, which reads, "Bring the full tithe into the storehouse, that there may be food in my house. And thereby put me to the test, says the LORD of hosts, if I will not open the windows of heaven for you and pour down for you a blessing until there is no more need" (ESV).

You see, 10 percent feels safe. But God's teaching on generosity goes well beyond what's safe. A family giving 10 percent of their income is doing wonders, yet probably isn't practicing radical generosity. However, a family giving 90 percent—I think you see where I'm headed here! You say it can't be done. Tell that to R. G. LeTourneau, an incredibly successful businessman of his time famous for living on 10 percent of his income and giving 90 percent to the spread of the gospel. He was fond of remarking, "It's not how much of my money I give to God, but how much of God's money I keep for myself."[37]

Of course, the actual percentage that your family ends up giving isn't the main point. The key question is: "What amount matches the level of generosity I've received from the Lord?" Keep in mind that the more your family steps out in faith with God's guidance, the more you will enter into that space of radical generosity. Remember that part of your leadership role is to push your family members outside of their comfort zones, to dig in and find ways to make the impossible possible when it comes to generosity.

3. I remember that the GO *phase is not always sequential or logical.* Things will happen. The baton will be dropped. You may even feel as though you're running backwards at times. Your personal mission statement and family mission statement are there to help you, but let's face it: life is complicated and difficult. Things don't always go according to plan.

My track coach taught us that when we were standing on the starting line, preparing for the starting gun to go off, we needed to keep our eyes focused on the track ahead and clear our minds of everything except the task before us. The Apostle Paul understood this when he wrote in Philippians 3:14, "I press on to reach the end of the race and receive the heavenly prize for which God, through Christ Jesus, is calling us" (NLT).

As the leader, your goal is to develop a multi-generational legacy of generosity. Your team needs you to show them how to accomplish this. But it's important to note that God's timetable may be different from yours. He cares more about you and your family than He does about your money and possessions. His ultimate goal is to transform each of you to become more like Him.

There may be times when it feels like you're not making progress, when the baton isn't being passed. In those times, allow God the space to work. Don't be so focused on the goal that you tune out the one voice that matters the most. God wants to change your life through this process, so let Him.

NARROW DOWN THE FIELD

I'll never forget when my family first sat down to brainstorm charities and causes to support. We came away with over twenty names. Twenty! Talk about feeling overwhelmed.

Each cause was worthy. Each was good and needed help. But we simply couldn't support them all in an impactful way. Since I was the leader, it was my role to reframe and bring focus to the conversation, so I took that long list and divided it into the following categories:

- The church/ evangelism

- Humanitarian relief

- Poverty

- Injustice

Then we assigned each category a percentage of our giving. It's important to acknowledge that your list may be different from my family's list. This is just to give you a glimpse into what this process looked like for us.

This new way to look at our list recharged discussion. We were able to narrow our selections and move forward with confidence and excitement.

Throughout this process, my wife and daughters often looked to me for guidance and perspective. I found it useful to remind myself that it was okay if I didn't have all of the answers. If I had all of the answers—or if you did for your family—then it would take the fun out of the process! As the heads of our families, as long as we're able to filter through the discussion and narrow in on what's important, our meetings will thrive.

It's normal to feel as though this is more than you can handle, but remember that God has you where He wants you, in complete reliance on Him. It's natural to fear that you won't have the answers when you need them or that you'll look foolish. We all face that! Rest assured that the right words will come as you work through the process together. This isn't a one-man or one-woman show. You need your team, and they need you—and you all need God's guidance more than ever. Jesus said, "I am the vine; you are the branches. Whoever abides in me and I in him, he it is that bears much fruit, for apart from me you can do nothing" (John 15:5 ESV).

Chapter Eight Notes

Fostering a Family Culture of Generosity

Let this be written for a future generation, that a people not yet created may praise the LORD....

—Psalm 102:18 *(NIV)*

I'm sure that there were times when my high school track coach felt as though he wasn't making progress. I'm sure that there were races after which his list of things for us to work on felt insurmountable. Yet he persisted, day by day, and our team dynamics changed over time. We got better. We got faster. We became more effective, more cohesive as a group. Eventually, we became a well-respected team that never gave up and competed well against the best.

Similarly, the process of a Legacy Continuum can be messy, because families are made up of messy people! No one is perfect, and progress can be difficult. It takes effort to work through family dynamics and underlying baggage. It takes trial and error to figure out how to communicate with everyone well. You're doing all of this while trying to create your family's legacy. It's a big responsibility to bear.

The good news is that as long as you're all focused on the finish line, on the goal, then you're going to make it through. You may not make it there in a straight line. You will certainly face unexpected obstacles and delays. But as long as you are working collectively toward the vision God has given you, you will run the race well, because He will "equip you with everything good for doing his will" (Hebrews 13:21 NIV).

How do you know that you're running the race well? When you have created a culture of generosity.

MODEL IT

Once, while Elina and I were in Dubai, UAE, we were returning to our apartment after dinner. In the elevator was an Arab couple who had gone grocery shopping. The husband was carrying a package of Arabic bread.

We had never seen this couple before, and after exchanging pleasantries, I commented on how wonderful the bread looked. Without any hesitation, he handed the package to me and offered it as a gift.

We were stunned at this act of generosity. Apparently, in Arab culture, if you admire a possession of your Arab host, he may feel obligated to offer it to you even if it is of special value to him.

Here's what stuck with me from that interaction. First, it showed me that there is a spontaneity to true generosity.

152

When we aren't living a life of generosity, we overthink things and second-guess ourselves. But for my newfound Arab friend, generosity was automatic.

Second, it showed me that generosity is learned. He wouldn't have done what he did if it hadn't already been a part of his life and family culture. Giving so quickly and freely was as natural to him as breathing. He had seen his parents and grandparents do this, and it was part of who he was.

A family culture of generosity can only be developed one family member at a time, and it starts when we change *who we are*. To make that change, we need two things: the *desire* to change and the *power* to change. For believers, the desire to change comes from within, but the sustaining power we need to change can come only from the work of the Holy Spirit. After all, "it is God who works in you, both to will and to work for his good pleasure" (Philippians 2:13 ESV).

When we focus on true generosity, when we make it part of who we are and how we live, it will soon become as automatic for us as it was for the stranger who, without a moment of hesitation, gave me bread off his table. Then our lives today will shape the lives of our children, grandchildren, and further down the line, resulting in true, lasting Kingdom impact.

Where do we begin? How do we help our families to live out a culture of active generosity? I have a few ideas.

1. Model it with stories from the past and present. I've written at length about how our ancestral stories shape us, and they play a key role in modeling a family culture of generosity.

During the summers when I was growing up, I worked in the Chinese restaurant that my dad managed. I remember that one of his responsibilities was to drive the waiters and cooks to Chinatown after closing. In those days, Manhattan's Chinatown was a bustling place late at night. Restaurant workers from around the city would go there after work to do their grocery shopping, get haircuts, grab a midnight snack, catch up on the news, and more.

Even though times were tough in those days for immigrants, my dad would not hesitate to invite the people he bumped into on the streets of Chinatown for tea or coffee. Witnessing these exchanges between immigrants who were barely eking out a living shaped me. It showed the importance of community and how generosity isn't just measured in dollars and cents. It's a state of mind, a way of life.

Stories like this from the past can be used to model a culture of generosity, and so can stories from the present. When you see a family member demonstrating generosity, acknowledge it! Tell the others! By calling attention to and celebrating the good things you see in one another, you'll promote a culture of generosity.

2. Model it by sharing your unique views of generosity. Each person in your family has a slightly different idea of what generosity looks like. This is because God speaks to each of us in a unique way. The visions He gives to one person are different from the visions He gives to another person.

You can model this by having each family member draw or write out what generosity looks like to him or her. This activity will give you incredible insight into one another. When you share these intimate details with one another, you'll come away stronger and more unified. It's not the final picture or diagram that matters. It's the richness of discussion, the vulnerability, and the time spent getting to know and learning from one another.

3. Model it by documenting the journey. When COVID-19 hit, I realized that how we were implementing our family plan of generosity didn't fit with what was happening in the world. We needed to pivot and respond to the pandemic while remaining true to our legacy mission. After much family discussion and input, the following diagram was created:

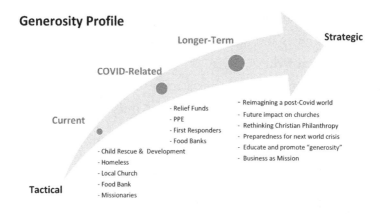

Generosity Profile

Strategic
- Reimagining a post-Covid world
- Future impact on churches
- Rethinking Christian Philanthropy
- Preparedness for next world crisis
- Educate and promote "generosity"
- Business as Mission

Longer-Term

COVID-Related
- Relief Funds
- PPE
- First Responders
- Food Banks

Current
- Child Rescue & Development
- Homeless
- Local Church
- Food Bank
- Missionaries

Tactical

The above "Generosity Profile" captured part of our generosity story at a particular moment in time. Specifically, we drew it in 2020 in response to the COVID-19 pandemic, which had caused our family to refine our approach to generosity.

If you're considering creating your own generosity profile, keep in mind that your generosity story will likely evolve over time. Suffice it to say that when you take the time to tell and show your generosity story, you will find that God will reward your efforts. He will deepen your understanding of generosity and show you how you can better align with His plan. The goal isn't a well-developed graphic. The goal is to talk about what has happened and where you're going and to document your journey.

4. Model it by looking at more than just the facts. We've already made the point that generosity is, by and large, a heart matter. Because of that, these family discussions are more than just facts and figures; they should include feelings and emotions as well.

As you grow together as a team, the questions you ask should become deeper. Consider such questions as:

- How do you feel when you are being generous?

- How does God fit into your giving?

- Why did you give to that organization or ministry?

- How do you want future generations to describe your generosity?

Diving into these topics can help to create a culture of generosity as you connect on an emotional level with the legacy work that you are all doing.

EXPLORE IT

Christian Smith's Science of Generosity initiative at the University of Notre Dame states, "Generosity ... is a learned character trait.... Generosity is therefore not a random idea or haphazard behavior but rather, in its mature form, a basic, personal, moral orientation to life. ... Generosity always intends to enhance the true wellbeing of those to whom it gives. What exactly generosity gives can be various things: money, possessions, time, attention, aid, encouragement, emotional availability, and more."[38]

Much like the stranger who gave me bread without a moment's hesitation, acting from learned behavior, we, too, can learn to be more generous. There are unlimited resources to help with this, but here are some of my favorites.

1. The Bible: You don't have to be a Bible scholar to lead your family through a study of what the Bible teaches on the subject of generosity. It doesn't need to be a lengthy, exegetical study. Small, bite-sized segments interspersed into your calendar year would be a great start to enlighten your team on how God views generosity.

For example, take the Apostle Paul's first letter to the church in Corinth. In it, he encouraged the church to collect an offering to help the believers in Jerusalem. Paul wrote, "Regarding the relief offering for poor Christians that is being collected, you get the same instructions I gave the churches in Galatia. Every Sunday each of you make an offering and put it in safekeeping. Be as generous as you can. When I get there you'll have it ready, and I won't have to make a special appeal" (1 Corinthians 16:1–2 MSG).

In reading this passage with your family, you could ask them what principles of generosity they see. To get them started, you could share the following observations:

- Our giving should be done on a regular and consistent basis, not just for special events or circumstances.

- Our generosity shouldn't be sourced only from our surplus; it should also be about giving sacrificially.

- Our generosity is intrinsically linked—some might even say directly proportional—to our love for God and others.

Many more insights will come as a result of your discussion. As you use Scripture to learn about generosity, you will be more easily able to challenge your team to put words into action.

- How will you carry out the message of this verse?

- What decisions need to be made in order to move forward in your giving journey?

- How do time, talent, and treasure play into the above passage?

These are just some of the questions you can pose once your team has unpacked a scripture like the one found in 1 Corinthians.

2. Generous Giving: If you're uncertain about developing mini studies to help your family learn about generosity, you could rely on an organization like Generous Giving.[39] They sponsor Journeys of Generosity (JOG), which are free online retreats for groups of like-minded people who are looking to maximize their Kingdom impact and fully live by the spirit of generosity.

3. National Christian Foundation (NCF):[40] This organization's website provides a great library of resources on the topic of generosity. Spending time reading their articles and taking in their information would certainly move you forward in your family's quest to learn about generosity.

4. Dave Ramsey:[41] His name is almost synonymous with personal finance and for good reason. Dave has helped countless people to get out of debt and live in financial freedom. As your family grows in their legacy, they will begin to see the importance of a solid budget and a debt-free life. Dave Ramsey's resources are great for improving your financial literacy.

5. Science of Generosity Initiative:[42] If your family appreciates a more scientific approach to the importance of generosity, then this resource is a great place to start. This initiative uses active research from the University of Notre Dame to dig into how our culture views generosity, and it explores critical questions, such as why people don't give more.

6. The Ron Blue Institute:[43] This resource is wonderful for helping you to integrate your faith into your personal finances, your life calling, and many other areas of life.

RESEARCH IT

While "Model It" and "Explore It" have to do with understanding and growing in generosity, the phases from here on out refer to the hard work of digging in and *doing* generosity. While it's nice to talk about and understand your legacy goal, it's more important to put actions to your words. *Doing* is what will create a culture of generosity within your family.

This is where the hard work of determining what causes, ministries, and nonprofit organizations will receive your family's time, talent, and treasure begins. As you look at your generosity profile, you can assess where you are as a family and begin to ask these tough questions:

- Why are we supporting these organizations? How effective is the organization in using our donations?

- Do these organizations fall in line with our family mission statement? If not, why are we keeping them on the list?

- How can we increase our total giving?

- Are there other organizations that we should support?

These questions are not merely for lip service or to check boxes as you hold your family meetings. They should force you to get your hands dirty and really think about what you're doing and why. It's an opportunity for your family to open up and share their thoughts. What engages them? What excites them? What is God saying to them? Those discussions are invaluable!

A year or two down the line, when you get to the point where your family members naturally open up and share and they come to meetings knowing what God is telling them, you'll find that you don't even need much of an agenda. You won't need many prompts because you will have created a culture of generosity that is alive and active in the hearts of your family members. Your Legacy Continuum will be thriving.

OWN IT

It feels good writing a check to someone in need, doesn't it? Do you want to know why? You get a boost of endorphins while not having to do any of the work!

I've often said that writing a check is the easy part of generosity. To maximize your Kingdom impact, you'll have to go deeper. You'll have to *own it*.

Owning your generosity goes beyond tapping your

treasure. It may mean encroaching on your time and leveraging your talent. Remember this formula from Chapter One:

$$\text{Involvement} \times \text{Insight} \times \text{Resources} = \text{Kingdom Impact}$$

Involvement can come in the form of personally volunteering with the organization you're looking to support. *Insight* can be gained by researching the organization and by truly connecting with the leaders, staff, and other volunteers. This will help you to get a feel for the heartbeat of the organization and their level of commitment to the goal. Your *resources* include your time, talent, and treasure. *Kingdom Impact* is the extent to which God's love is shared through meeting the needs of others and changing lives.

Now take a closer look at the equation. Think of an organization on your heart. Assuming that this organization is effective in utilizing your donations, it's not just the money that will increase its Kingdom impact, but also your involvement and deeper understanding of the organization and its leaders. All of those things together add up to produce a much greater impact than if you were simply writing a check.

Several years ago, I was invited to an angel investing meeting. This is a type of investing that helps startups, new businesses, and small firms to receive the funding they need in exchange for shares or equity in the company. The individuals who participate in this type of investing are called angel investors. For a guy like me, this type of meeting is exhilarating!

During my first meeting, two companies presented. I remember noting how well done their presentations were. Each was focused on convincing the audience *why* they should invest in the company. They talked about their leadership, their business plan, and their finances. They cast a vision for how they were going to disrupt the marketplace with their product or service.

It was truly an inspiring experience, and I remember coming away from that wondering why we didn't use the same method during our family meetings. I thought about how much the dynamic of our meetings would shift if we were to come to the table armed and ready to make a case as to why we should support a certain cause.

You see, the individuals presenting at that angel meeting believed fully in their business. They *owned* it and became evangelists for its success. Your family can own it, too. You can foster this by asking family members to find, research, and present an organization that they feel passionate about. Instruct them to communicate a clear ask. How much time, talent, and treasure do they want set aside for their organization, and how do they envision it being put to use? What will be accomplished, and how will this disrupt the world for the Kingdom? This may come more easily to the natural salespeople and leaders in your family, but you'd be surprised what a passionate heart can do when so much is on the line!

As always, keep God in the middle of these conversations.

This may be a businesslike approach, but it's not a business decision. This is a God decision. He calls the shots as He moves in your hearts.

SHARE IT

Finally, a family culture of generosity won't be able to stop telling others about the incredible change that has happened in hearts and lives. Whenever I'm sharing with family, friends, and even strangers what I'm up to, I always find a way to talk about how our family meets on a regular basis to talk about how we can do generosity better together. The reaction I get is almost universal. Their eyes light up. They want to learn more, and I'm happy to tell them! Sadly, most people are amazed that families even do this sort of thing, but with God's help, you can make it happen in your family.

In a wonderful way, these kinds of conversations encouraged me to appear as a guest on a podcast for the first time. Kyle Gillette is a friend of mine, and during one of our regular coffee meetups, he asked me what I was working on. Before I knew it, he had invited me on his SAGE Mindset Podcast. Kyle had never heard anyone talk about legacy with such intentionality, and he was intrigued by some of my key ideas relating to family legacies, radical generosity, and Kingdom impact—all of which I've expanded upon in this book.

I have Kyle to thank because he challenged me to go deeper and find ways of sharing my journey of generosity with others to inspire them to do the same. By sharing our experiences and what we're learning, we become a blessing to others. God never intended for the change happening within us to be subtle or to go unnoticed. Matthew 5:16 says, "Let your light so shine before men, that they may see your good works, and glorify your Father which is in heaven" (KJV). God wants others to notice as your family moves toward generosity. He wants them to ask questions, and He wants you to be bold in sharing.

Remember that the end goal is Kingdom impact. The more families who do this, the greater the collective impact will be, the more hearts will change, and the more generosity will become part of our Christian culture. Imagine how your example could encourage other families to create their own Legacy Continuum. This is about building up the body of Christ and equipping believers in the faith. Much like one flame can light an infinite number of candles, your quest for a Kingdom-focused legacy can ignite the desire within others.

YOU'RE BLESSED TO BE A BLESSING

This process will be difficult. Reaching a point where your family creates a culture of generosity is no simple task. You won't get it right all of the time. You'll make mistakes, and I promise that it will take longer than you want it to. But I also promise you that God is in this and He will bless your efforts.

It's easy to praise God when we're on the mountaintop, when things are going well and plans fall into place. It's much harder to praise and trust Him in the valley, but that's exactly what is needed.

There is a reason that God is leading your family through this process. It's not just about being able to write a check to a worthy charity. It's not even about your personal involvement in a good cause. It's about what God will do in your heart and the hearts of your family members as you journey together. The blessing that will come from that is immeasurable.

When your family reaches a point where generosity is natural, when your hearts are tuned to the needs around you, when you're going about everyday tasks and cannot stop thinking about the Legacy Continuum, that is when the story of your family will change. That's when the legacy will live on. Everything it takes to get to that point is worth it.

Chapter Nine Notes

Setting Up Your Family for Success

*And let us not grow weary of doing good, for in due season
we will reap, if we do not give up.*
—Galatians 6:9 *(ESV)*

Family Partnership Meetings are the driving force behind
your Legacy Continuum. It's these meetings that will
determine your trajectory. In this chapter, I'm going to throw
a lot at you. I'm going to share details about these meetings
and what has worked for me, but I want to be clear about
something: your family is unique. What works for me may
not work for you. However, I believe that some of the
underlying principles will be invaluable in your planning and
leadership.

In one of our small groups we formed with long-term
friends, we'd never talked much about money, generosity,
and legacy. So when we decided to study those topics, I
wasn't sure what to expect. I knew that I would be leading
the group through the discussion, but how would God lead

and guide us? How would He move?

The experience has turned out to be an incredible blessing. For eight months, we met and talked and shared. We treated it much like a Family Partnership Meeting, the only differences being that we aren't related by blood and we aren't combining our efforts toward a joint legacy.

In this time together, people have changed. Their approach to money and legacy has changed. Some are living differently from how they lived eight months ago, and some are refocusing priorities.

The key is that each family has recognized that they need to do what's right for them. The race of generosity isn't about who's in the lead. It's not about following a certain meeting agenda or ticking boxes on a list. It's about gathering your team on the track and staying in the race.

As you begin your Family Partnership Meetings, it's essential to tailor them to your specific needs and family dynamics. This isn't about copying and pasting everything I've written, and there certainly isn't going to be a test later! This is about filtering what I'm sharing through the lens of your family. Please keep that in mind as we dive into the details of Family Partnership Meetings.

ESTABLISH THE BASICS

Because Family Partnership Meetings will be your primary vehicle for preparing your family to continue building on your Legacy Continuum, it's important to have some basic rules of thumb so that family members can set their expectations.

1. Meet regularly. My family started with annual meetings, but progress was slow and momentum was hard to come by. Right now, we're meeting monthly. While this works for us and where we are in our journey, monthly meetings can feel like a big commitment. I think that quarterly meetings are a great place to start. You can adjust as needed.

2. Make sure that everyone attends. Another thing that has proven to be a fundamental part of the process is to make sure that everyone can attend. You may have to reschedule a few times, and you may end up having to deal with some folks who are less interested than others in the process as a whole, but having the full team there will help you to get to the goal faster.

3. Be productive. In my forty-two years in corporate America, I've probably spent over 4,000 hours in meetings. And of those hours, I'm guessing that 1,500 were unproductive—unless I spent that time nodding off! Now don't get me wrong. I've led my share of unproductive meetings. When this happened, it was because:

- I didn't spend sufficient time thinking about and defining the purpose of the meeting.

- I didn't send out an agenda before the meeting (more on this later).

- I didn't exert strong leadership during the meeting by keeping us on course, handling conflict, and clarifying next steps (more on this later as well).

Meetings are important for any group effort. They can affirm the group and its mission, deepen relationships, hone leadership skills, invite God into the process, and so much more. For example, I typically start our meetings with prayer, asking God's Spirit for direction and guidance, and then end our meetings with a simple prayer of thanks. That prayer has morphed over time into an incredible time of praying for one another. There is no greater privilege than for parents to pray with their children. This is why it's imperative that you get your Family Partnership Meetings off to a good start. You want to encourage and energize your team, not bore them or waste their time.

ESTABLISH PURPOSE

Meetings without a clear purpose will quickly become casual gatherings during which very little of value is accomplished. Agendas are a great way to ensure productivity, and sending them out five to seven days before the meeting will allow attendees to pray and prepare before coming together.

As you create your agenda, keep two things in mind. First, welcome input from others. The agenda shouldn't just be *your* creation. Anyone in the group should be able to propose agenda items. Second, shape the agenda around the meeting's most critical purpose. This purpose may vary from meeting to meeting depending on how your team evolves and discussion shifts. You may ask yourself if the purpose of the meeting is:

- To reach a decision

- For the education and edification of the group

- To brainstorm a problem or the development of a plan of action

- For team building and bonding

- For taking a break from previous heavy discussions and keeping it light, or

- For sharing with and praying for one another.

LEADERSHIP BEST PRACTICES

A meeting without a leader will struggle to move from item to item, while a meeting led by a dictator will result in your team members either shying away from discussion or rebelling against you. The best leadership approach is to be interesting, educational, and engaging. Other things that I've learned over the years about leading meetings include the following:

1. Respect everyone's time. There's nothing more frustrating than the never-ending meeting, as most people have other things they need to do. Keep an eye on the time or assign someone else that role.

2. Know when to move on. If conflict or indecision enters the meeting, you'll need to be decisive to keep those things from taking control. It's important to allow other people to have opinions, but don't dwell on the differences and certainly don't let the distractions of the world dictate discussion. Politics, culture, the news of the day—these topics will inevitably come up, and it's important to acknowledge them. But it's also important to give them boundaries.

An example of this is when I brought up the topic of hate crimes against Asian Americans. I wanted to have a family discussion about it because it was something that was undoubtedly affecting all of us as Asian Americans, whether emotionally, mentally, or physically. However, I was sure to keep a tight leash on the discussion. Whenever we veered off topic, I brought us back, reminding us of the family mission and vision based on Luke 3:11.

Ultimately, the family determined that while we were affected by what was being done against the Asian American community, the topic was much too politically charged for us to make it a part of our legacy work. Our goal is to help the needy, the poor, and the helpless. We determined that we could do this without taking up that particular social justice banner at that particular moment. Instead, we added the topic to our "parking lot" and planned to revisit it periodically. Allowing the conversation to take place within set boundaries was a way for us to work through something that was very painful and still keep our eyes on the goal.

3. Find ways to engage and empower your team. At first, you'll probably do most of the talking, but for your team to grow and mature, they will need to participate in discussions and even take ownership of some of the agenda items.

4. Focus on the family unit and the future as opposed to individual wants and needs. Rally your team around the bigger picture of the Legacy Continuum, reminding them about the *why.*

5. Recognize that you don't need to have all of the answers now. If you find yourself stuck on a topic or a disagreement, set it aside and move on to things that will allow you to move forward in accomplishing your goals. You can always revisit topics in future meetings.

6. Practice the fruit of the Spirit as found in Galatians 5:22–23. Strive to demonstrate "love, joy, peace, patience, kindness, goodness, faithfulness, gentleness, [and] self-control" (ESV). Keep this front and center, especially if your family is one that tends to diverge and disagree more often than not.

7. Ensure that everyone has a role to play with defined responsibilities. Each person needs to feel needed and heard. You can accomplish that by assigning your family members roles and tasks based on their individual strengths, gifts, and passions.

8. Never underestimate the power of prayer. There's something special that happens when a family prays together.

If you ever face trouble leading the group, it may be time for some serious prayer.

9. Finally, when the meeting is over, send a follow-up email. Recap everything that was discussed, including next steps.

EXPECT THE UNEXPECTED

The immediate catalyst for my family's discussion about helping Asian American causes was a paper I came across by Asian Americans/ Pacific Islanders in Philanthropy (AAPIP), in which they shared that funding for causes relating to injustices to the broader Asian American community had been stagnant from 2009 to 2018. Nine years without growth would be a blow to any organization, but these particular causes were close to my heart.

My guess is that you, too, will find yourself confronted with a cause that's important to you, but you'll be at a loss as to how to proceed. This makes for a great discussion during a Family Partnership Meeting.

When I made this cause the focus of a Family Partnership Meeting, my agenda was simple. I linked to the paper and asked my family to read it beforehand, and I posed three questions.

- Question 1: What did you get out of this paper? Does it make a good case for their causes?

- Question 2: Should our family use its resources to support this organization?

- Question 3: Will supporting this organization be consistent with our family's giving mission?

This topic connected with my family as Asian Americans. We had a fruitful discussion, and while we concluded that this particular organization wasn't the best fit for us, we continued to look for similar organizations.

Our research proved to be frustrating. Most of the organizations we uncovered had a political agenda—something that could be good and helpful, but it wasn't in line with our Family Mission Statement. We knew that we needed to think outside the box. Scripture is replete with God's command to help others and care for the poor; there was no question about that. But *how*? If there isn't clear direction, it's okay to table a discussion, but in this case, we were able to pivot.

As we brainstormed how to move forward, I listened carefully to how each family member was being led by the Holy Spirit. I opened myself up to their ideas and allowed each of them to go through a self-discovery process as we sought God and what He wanted.

It was then that we began to ask ourselves: Do we really need a buffer between us and the needy at all? Why not go directly to the people we want to help? We wanted to find something that aligned with our family mission statement, so we reread it:

Two Tunics Legacy is an expression of God's abounding generosity. Our mission is to live out and promote the call to action in Luke 3:11. We do this by engaging, challenging, and partnering with others to visibly demonstrate the power of God's provision and compassion to a world in need.

After we reacquainted ourselves with our family mission statement, one of my daughters came up with a guiding question: What if we directly support fellow Christians who have dreams of restoring and renewing a broken world but don't have the financial means or network to do so?

Our daughter had experience working with a nonprofit that was equipping believers to pursue their dreams of Kingdom work. Through the Goldenwood organization, she had witnessed firsthand the power of a community that shares this common vision and passionately collaborates toward that end, enlivened by the Spirit, the very breath of God.

After much discussion, we agreed that we needed to talk with this nonprofit. We set up a meeting with them and quickly found that we were in alignment. We worked with them to shape a unique program that would pair our funding and goals with the nonprofit's strengths. The result was The Dream Forum, which I mentioned in Chapter Seven.

The Dream Forum invites people to bring their big ideas to the table. From there, qualified experts weigh in, curating the top, most compelling proposals. We identified eight top visions, and our family foundation provided funding along with connections and resources to allow each one to move from an idea to reality. The eight visions range from a home for children who have aged out of foster care to a place of rest and renewal for those in the entertainment field. Each of the eight ideas follows my family's mission to help renew and restore a broken world, listening to the Spirit of God as we do so.

Being a part of The Dream Forum has been an incredible experience and blessing for our family. This type of project wasn't even on our radar before! If you would have asked me at the beginning of my family's legacy journey what type of work we would be doing, my response would not have come close to touching on the work we're doing through The Dream Forum. I'm an engineer. I like things that are concrete, with the details all figured out. Something like The Dream Forum would have seemed too abstract for a mind like mine.

When you let go of control and you let the meeting do what it's supposed to do, the only thing you can expect is the unexpected. God had to work on me to open me up. I had to trust Him instead of leaning on my own understanding (Proverbs 3:5–6). The result has been an incredible blessing not only to the people who have received help, but also to me.

CREATE A FAMILY RHYTHM

You may be sold on the idea of conducting regular family meetings to focus on generosity and legacy, but you may also be wondering what an agenda would look like and if it would be interesting enough to excite and attract the attention of your family members. Again, each family should take an approach that works for them, but it may be useful for me to share an example of what my family meeting agendas look like. It will at least provide you with a framework that you can modify to suit your family's needs.

1. Prayer and a quiet pause. We acknowledge God's presence and rightful place in our family and in the meeting. Then we take a moment of stillness and silence, asking God to focus and prepare our minds and hearts with an expectation of revelation from Him. This puts us in the right state of mind and reminds us that God is at the center of our legacy.

If you're already praying together as a family, this time shouldn't be difficult. But if you're not used to praying or even being still before God as a family, then this may be a bit uncomfortable at first. A time of quiet can be unsettling, but that is when God moves and works. You will find that He speaks to you and others in those quiet moments.

You'll also find that by starting out the meeting this way, you'll be better able to shut out all of the minor distractions so you can focus on the only One who matters and on the direction He has for you and your family. As the leader, you can offer an opening prayer, read a short devotional, or simply share a Bible verse that is particularly meaningful to you.

2. Learning generosity together. The purpose of a group discussion is to center our family on the topic of generosity, to engage in an open dialogue, to learn generosity together, and for everyone to get on the same page. It is also a time to discuss any struggles or uncertainty team members may have about the principles of God's generosity.

There are many ways that I've found to help this conversation along. One recommendation I have is to use *The Treasure Principle* by Randy Alcorn. He lays out the following treasure principles and gives the appropriate scripture that will lead to a fruitful discussion. To give you a taste, here are the treasure principles:[44]

> *God owns everything. I'm His money manager.* We are the managers of the assets God has entrusted—not given—to us.
>
> *My heart always goes where I put God's money.* Watch what happens when you reallocate your money from temporal things to eternal things.
>
> *Heaven and the future new earth, not this fallen one, is my home.* We are citizens of "a better country—a heavenly one" (Hebrews 11:16).
>
> *Should live not for the dot but for the line.* From the dot—our present life on Earth—extends a line that goes on forever, which is eternity in Heaven.
>
> *Giving is the only antidote to materialism.* Giving is a joyful surrender to a greater person and a greater agenda. It dethrones me and exalts Him.
>
> *God prospers me not to raise my standard of living but to raise my standard of giving.* God gives us more money than we need so we can give—generously.

It's important not to tackle all of the above treasure principles in one Family Partnership Meeting. It may take you a year to get through them all, and that's okay. Bite off as much as the group can chew. I cited several other resources earlier in this book, and there are many more available as well.

3. Transfer of wealth and riches. For this agenda item, my wife and I spend time sharing advice and wisdom for the next generation. The goal is to share family stories that exemplify the values, beliefs, practices, and knowledge that previous generations have cultivated within our family as well as the wisdom that my wife and I have attained throughout our lives. This gives the next generation a much greater chance at success.

Very few families develop plans to preserve and pass on their assets. Furthermore, only three percent of people have written financial goals. If you're thinking of what to discuss in a Family Partnership Meeting about passing on wealth and riches, consider questions such as:

- What has God taught you about money and finances?

- What is the difference between inherent wealth and riches?

- What did you learn from your parents' generation and family about money (the good, the bad, and the ugly)?

- What are the core beliefs and practices that you have tried to live by regarding the handling of inherent wealth and riches?

- Share your estate plan, last will and testament, durable power of attorney for financial matters, healthcare directive, and so on. Go into as much detail as you're comfortable with. My wife and I have chosen not to share any of our financial information. The overall goal is to share your thoughts about why these things are important and what you are trying to accomplish. This will create a spirit of transparency and will prevent any surprises after you're gone. These discussions will also help your children when they eventually think through their own long-term planning.

- How do you do financial planning? Our children are all highly intelligent, but we shouldn't assume that they know it all. Through these discussions, you will get a sense of how financially savvy your children are. There are an infinite number of resources, some of which I cited earlier, to help them better understand the nuts and bolts of managing their finances. We can learn more from our mistakes than from our successes, so even if you have botched up your finances, your children can learn from your missteps.

- What are your dreams for your children? Your grandchildren? Future generations? How do you want to help them financially and spiritually?

- What legacy do you want to leave?

4. Revisiting the family mission. This part of the meeting is your opportunity to reimagine and fortify the basic principles relating to your family's generosity and legacy mission and then ensure that those principles get passed down. This is not about spending hours re-crafting your mission statement.

My family and I often spend this time asking ourselves questions like:

- What are the guiding principles that have sustained us over the years?

- What do we stand for?

- How different will the mission be for our children's families?

5. Developing family giving projects. This is my favorite part of our meetings. We get to learn about what God is saying to each of us, the desires and dreams of how we can bring renewal and restoration to a broken and needy world. From here, we discuss if we want to take on a new project together or simply support one another in our individual efforts. For part of this process, we use the Angel Funding method, in which each family member brings a potential idea to the table. Then, as a family, we decide which ideas to pursue.

6. Praying for one another. As important as all of the above topics are, this part is the most rewarding. We have found that the more specific we are with our requests, the more impactful our prayers will be. We ask each other about marital relationships, personal struggles, family issues, and other sensitive topics. The only off-limit topics are politics and news from the world. Of course, this is something that has taken my family years to navigate. We had to ease into it, and your family may have to do the same.

Being still together in prayer is a way for you to bond as a family and to reflect on the needs of the individual family members, what they're going through and struggling with, and the life circumstances that they're carrying with them as they enter into this time together.

The six-item sample agenda above is the result of years of honing my Family Partnership Meeting agenda-making skills, and it has been effective for my family. After much trial and error, we have finally found an agenda system that works for us, and the same will happen for your family, too.

BE FLEXIBLE AND TRUST GOD

As you begin the Family Partnership Meeting journey, I encourage you to try different approaches to see what works best for your family. Be flexible and ask for discernment. I believe that God will meet you in your desire for a Legacy Continuum. He will show you the way.

Family Partnership Meetings have become a place where my family can be ambitious, seek God, and build legacy. Our topics of discussion are unique to us, and we don't shy away from tackling difficult issues. The conversations we have are not always easy, but they are necessary. I'm very proud of how far we've come together, but don't for a moment think that your family can't also reach this point.

After a big high school track meet, my coach would gather

us together to discuss what went well and what we could do differently next time. Family Partnership Meetings are your chance to recalibrate, to try new things, to critique existing practices, and to become better, together, in your race for Kingdom impact. Through it all, trust that God will guide you and show you the best path forward for your family.

Chapter Ten Notes

Passing My Baton

This may feel like a lot of information—and it is—but I assure you that if you stick with it, your family will soon find its stride. Yes, it took me many years to find a method that worked. My prayer is that what I've shared in this book will help you to accomplish even more on your journey.

When you do reach a point where things are moving forward and the kinks are worked out, you'll be surprised by all that you'll be able to accomplish with your family, your team. Running this race with my family has informed and established everything I've written in this book.

With that in mind, I would like to leave you with the following reminders to carry with you as you live your life to leave a lasting legacy:

1. Your legacy isn't just about you. God has given you a legacy worth living, and He wants to work through you to impact others for His purposes. A crucial part of doing this is setting your heart to love God: "'You must love the Lord your God with all your heart, with all your soul, and with all your mind.' This is the greatest and most important commandment. The second is exactly like it: 'You must love your neighbor as yourself'" (Matthew 22:37–39 ISV). Your legacy is informed by those who have come before you, and it is enriched by living your legacy purposefully in the present with the support of your loved ones.

2. Develop a lasting legacy based on radical generosity. Be intentional about the legacy you want to leave based on your faith in God and your commitment to His Son, Jesus Christ. Start by developing a personal mission statement. Ensure that your mission statement is born from a desire to follow and obey Jesus. If we love God, we will obey Christ's commands by copying His example (John 14:15). Loving Jesus is not merely a feeling; it is an active, abiding, ongoing relationship based on following and obeying Him. This reality continues to shape us.

Lead your family in developing a family mission around radical generosity in order to help renew and restore a broken and needy world. This will enable you to be an example for future generations. You can remind, teach, and demonstrate to future generations your commitment to practicing radical generosity as an obedient steward of God's blessings. You can demonstrate your love for God by loving His people. This includes serving the needy, the poor, and the disadvantaged and sharing the love of God with those who don't know Him. This focus keeps us on track.

Another way to exemplify radical generosity is by standing

against injustice. For my family, this looks like striving to honor our mixed racial heritage and never forgetting the sacrifices made and the injustices suffered by our ancestors who first immigrated to America. Commit to speaking out against injustice in whatever area God directs you.

Determine how you and your family will utilize your collective time, talent, and treasure for the benefit of God's kingdom on earth. Hold yourselves accountable.

3. Exercise your God-given superpower to impact the future. Fight for the future of your family! Love them, engage them, and give them a vision for the future. As you move toward this goal, be aware of the devil's agenda. He commands powerful forces in the world, physical and spiritual, and his mission is to dismantle the family unit. We must resist the devil and his mission! Band together and show the world what it looks like when members of a family are committed to each other with unconditional love and a passion for the Lord's work.

With this in mind, work hard at establishing a solid financial foundation to help sustain your Legacy Continuum. Financial resources can be used as a force for good to help restore and renew a broken world. Allow God to lead you to the right causes and charities to invest in as you use the assets He has given you to benefit His kingdom.

Equip and train your family to run this race for the long term, and position them for a successful handoff of the legacy baton to the next generation. Having a strong financial foundation is partly for the purpose of investing in future generations. This means contributing to the education and edification of those who will follow you and eventually assume leadership of your family's Legacy Continuum. In other words, prepare future generations to take the baton handed to them and to pass it along successfully.

You can begin demonstrating radical generosity now! Develop a family rhythm for practicing it. Pass on the gift that keeps giving for generations, well into the future.

The reminders above are ultimately the culmination of the legacy my heavenly Father has provided me. In the beginning of this book, we discussed a spiritual will and observed Moses expressing his blessings for his sons. Well, this book and these principles are my expressed blessings, given to me by God, for future generations. This book is intended to change the trajectory of your life and the lives of all the generations that will come from you.

May reading this book be your first step in intentionally establishing your own Legacy Continuum. With the Lord guiding your steps, you can trust Him to empower you and your family to carry a baton of radical generosity and Kingdom impact to future generations. I'm passing the baton to you! Now take it and run your race well.

Afterwords by Vanessa Leong and Vivian Cruz

A WORD FROM VANESSA LEONG

In my favorite fictional stories, there is a young, inexperienced but promising hero-to-be (think Frodo, Moana, and the Karate Kid). This character starts out naive, perhaps weak, and is destined to stay that way, but for the wizened elder who puts the apprentice through his or her paces. Usually, those paces involve routines, habits, and exercises that the apprentice sees as useless and silly, but by trusting the process, the hero-to-be grows in strength and wisdom.

If I think of God as the "wizened elder" to my family as the apprentice, I am awed at the process we've had to trust. So little of what we did in the beginning was strategically thought out, but it turns out, God was putting us through our paces.

In 2007, I helped start a nonprofit called Many Hopes as

a passion project. I ran the organization's first fundraiser and asked my family to contribute. I can't remember what we gave—probably less than $1,000 —and I was only focused on making a dent in the overall $20,000 fundraising goal. It was one of the first grants our family made, and it was made believing in Many Hopes' long-term view of investing in children to become changemakers. We didn't know it then, but the principle of investing for the long run, for the generations, would become a core value for Two Tunics. A decade and a half later, Many Hopes has grown to be a $2 million organization that works in six countries, and Two Tunics has funded multiple organizations that share our heart for generational change.

One of the greatest joys of my life has been this generosity journey—to have played a small part in Many Hopes and to have helped shape Two Tunics. But there are so many turning points where things could have played out differently. As a family, we could have waited until Two Tunics had a rock-solid strategy and clearly defined responsibilities, and for us to have clear guidance from God, before moving. Or, we could have waited for Many Hopes to be a more established organization instead of a ragtag (but passionate) group of volunteers in their mid-twenties. We could have bailed out, unwilling to let Many Hopes or Two Tunics go through growing pains. I could have missed out on all of this. But persistence pays off, and by God's grace, I've enjoyed the privilege and deep satisfaction of giving money away and seeing what God does with it.

So, to anyone nervous or unsure about this journey, I

encourage you to trust the process! You won't have all the answers. We didn't. We still don't. But I find reassurance in the words God said to Joshua at the edge of the promised land: "I will give you every place where you set your foot" (Joshua 1:3 NIV). God wants us to step out actively—and He'll take care of the rest. A precise map, all the equipment, and an immovable strategy are not prerequisites to getting started. All we have to do is love God, love others, and take a first step. The generosity journey is simpler and more joyful than we might think. I hope you'll step out, too, and enjoy the ride.

A WORD FROM VIVIAN CRUZ

Being the youngest daughter, and certainly taking my fair share of twists and turns along the way, I've often struggled to find my place in the family. When we had our first family meeting to discuss Two Tunics and our family legacy, my initial thoughts went to the financial aspects of inheritance and giving. However, as a full-time mother, and an unpaid household general manager juggling the variables that come with being a military spouse, I've always known that making major financial contributions to our family legacy would never be my role. The question is, then: what can I do to impact our family's Legacy Continuum?

I often reflect on the experiences and obstacles my parents, and their parents before them, have overcome to improve the lives of future generations. I can't help but feel a burden of responsibility to show my appreciation and do my part as well. And I often do not feel up to the task. Even as sit here now, in the chaos of my household, past the deadline for writing this short piece (sorry, Dad!), I hear the ever-present echoes of "Mom, I'm hungry," and, "What was that password?" filtering through my noise-cancelling headphones, and I struggle to think of what I could possibly add to the reader's experience.

So, tapping into the resources on hand, I sought the advice of my seven-year-old. When I asked him what kind of legacy he wants to pass on to his future kids, after getting past his initial answers of teaching them about Super Mario and eating good food, he landed on a simple but important concept: *teach them to love God*.

Considering all the content, wisdom, and challenges this book presents, I realize my son's answer—speaking to the love of God—brings it all together for me. While I am still navigating how to use my resources, no matter how limited I feel some of them may be, I know that I want to pass on the godly love that my parents have always shown me. My parents are able to challenge, but not overwhelm. They will rebuke and correct, but always through the lens of love and grace. They have shown such a commitment and intentionality in generosity. And they are ever-present and involved in my family's life. As a parent myself now, I can see how they have managed their time, talents, and treasure not only to impact areas of God's kingdom, but also to set me up for my own successes.

Modeling and teaching the fundamentals of what I've learned from my parents, and what my dad has diligently translated into this book to share with others, is a role that I know God has called my husband and I to fill within our family's Legacy Continuum. Any limitations I feel in my own resources does not minimize the impact I can have on my own children right now. And I can't help but be excited to see how God will multiply the heart for a lasting generosity from our collective and intentional efforts as a family!

Acknowledgments

Going alone was never my thing. I knew from an early age that I was always meant to be a part of a team. I've always achieved my very best on a team, and I've received my greatest rewards as a team player. This book became reality only because of the incredibly generous and gifted team that only God could provide.

I'm extremely thankful for my loving wife and life-long partner, Elina, who sacrificially and graciously provided me the freedom to pursue my dreams and aspirations, even the misguided ones, for nearly half a century.

I'm humbled by my daughters, Vanessa and Vivian, who have so willingly accepted my imperfect parental leadership, for being committed sojourners on our family journey of generosity. The future of our family legacy is in good hands. Also, I'm so grateful to each of you for lending your voice to this book.

My deepest thanks to my friends and fellow Board members at the National Christian Foundation Northwest, who taught me so much about the intersection of wealth and generosity through words, resources, and especially, their lives. I greatly appreciate Kendra VanderMeulen, who so willingly and graciously offered to write the foreword to this book, for being an exceptional servant-leader.

I'm grateful for the incredible folks at Generous Giving, who provided the seminal event in our family's journey of generosity. Thank you, April Chapman, for your encouragement and leadership. You always inspire others to be better!

I appreciate Heather Tuininga for her invaluable feedback and influence, which goes beyond this book. You are a great inspiration to those of us still learning how to do generosity.

It is not practical for me to list the many people God sent to me during this long journey who have inspired me, encouraged me, and kept me going. Special thanks to Kyle Gillette, Terry Smith, Joe Eelkema and so many others who will never know the extent of their influence on me and this book.

I'm deeply grateful to all who took the time to read my manuscript and graced it with their testimonials and endorsements.

This project would not have been possible without the assistance of the many people who helped me through the writing, editing, and publishing process. Heartfelt thanks to Caleb Breakey and his entire team at *Speak It To Book*. They stuck with me the entire way and were instrumental in getting this book across the finish line. A special shoutout to my main reviewers—Kyle Gillette, Brian Steele, and Vanessa Leong—for their insightful and thoughtful feedback. I've learned so much from each of you.

Finally, the driving force behind this book comes from my

grandsons, Jayden and Jaxon, and from the many generations yet to come. May your past help equip you to have a God-sized impact on a world that desperately needs your voice.

About the Author

RICHARD LEONG spent most of his forty-two-year professional life as a "corporate nomad" living, working, and traveling throughout six different continents, thus mastering the art of maximizing travel rewards. During his spherical career, he held several key executive positions in premier equipment and technology companies in the energy sector.

Now living in Bellingham, Washington, Richard is actively leveraging his faith and corporate experience within the church, nonprofit organizations, and the local community. He is the managing director of Two Tunics Legacy Fund, a family foundation, and he cofounded Renewal Philanthropy. He also serves on the boards of National Christian Foundation Northwest and Illuminate NW.

Richard and his wife, Elina, are very proud of their two daughters, son-in-law, and two very active grandsons, and they are committed to creating a multi-generational legacy of generosity for their family.

About Renown Publishing

Renown Publishing was founded with one mission in mind: to make your great idea famous.

At Renown Publishing, we don't just publish. We work hard to pair strategy with innovative marketing techniques so that your book launch is the start of something bigger.

Learn more at <u>RenownPublishing.com</u>.

Notes

1. Deloitte. "The Deloitte Global 2021 Millennial and Gen Z Survey." 2021. https://www2.deloitte.com/global/en/pages/about-deloitte/articl es/millennialsurvey.html.

2. PwC. "Millennials at Work: Reshaping the Workplace." 2011. https://www.pwc.com/co/es/publicaciones/assets/millennials-at-work.pdf.

3. American Dictionary of the English Language, "wealth." By Noah Webster, Chauncey Allen Goodrich, and Joseph Emerson Worcester, *An American Dictionary of the English Language: Exhibiting the Origin, Orthography, Pronunciation, and Definitions of Words*. S. Converse, 1828. https://webstersdictionary1828.com/Dictionary/wealth.

4. Webster, Goodrich, and Worcester, *An American Dictionary*, p. 649.

5. Williams, Michael L. "How Does the Bible Define Wealth?" Christian Crier. December 31, 2014.

6. Hall, Mark. "The Greatest Wealth Transfer in History: What's Happening and What Are the Implications." Forbes. November 11, 2019. https://www.forbes.com/sites/markhall/2019/11/11/the-greatest

-wealth-transfer-in-history-whats-happening-and-what-are-the-implica tions/?sh=403a17c14090.

7. Kleinhandler, David. "Generational Wealth: Why Do 70% of Families Lose Their Wealth in the 2nd Generation?" Nasdaq. https://www. nasdaq.com/articles/generational-wealth%3A-why-do-70-of-families-lose-their-wealth-in-the-2nd-generation-2018–10.

8. Hirst, J., and M. Hirst. "What Is Kingdom Impact?" Innovation in Mission. February 19, 2007. https://innovationinmission.blogspot.com/ 2007/02/what-is-kingdom-impact.html.

9. Taylor, Philip R. "We Do Not Find God; God Finds Us." Faithlife. https://sermons.faithlife.com/sermons/26386-we-do-not-find-god-god-finds-us.

10. Know Your Southern History. "Paul 'Bear' Bryant." http://www. knowsouthernhistory.net/Biographies/Bear_Bryant/.

11. Stanley, C. F. *The Charles F. Stanley Life Principles Bible*. Nelson Bibles, 2005. https://biblestudyforlife.wordpress.com/2011/06/02/how -does-god-define-wealth/.

12. Gladwell, Malcolm. *Outliers: The Story of Success*. Little, Brown, 2008.

13. Stanley, Andy. *The Principle of the Path*. Thomas Nelson, 2011.

14. Roddenberry, Gene. *Star Trek: The Next Generation*. Paramount Domestic Television, 1987–1994.

15. Roddenberry, *Star Trek*.

16. Andrews, Andy. "Your Personal Mission Statement Action Plan." 2016. https://www.andyandrews.com/wp-content/uploads/Your-Personal-Mission-Statement-Action-Plan-by-Andy-Andrews.pdf.

17. Coenn, Daniel. *Abraham Lincoln: His Words*. BookRix, 2014.

18. Merriam Webster, "train." https://www.merriam-webster.com/dictionary/train.

19. Ansberry, Clare. "The Questions You Wish You Had Asked Your Parents." Wall Street Journal. March 2, 2020. https://www.wsj.com/articles/the-questions-you-wish-you-had-asked-your-parents-11583067601.

20. National Christian Foundation. "Generosity Library." https://www.ncfgiving.com/library/.

21. Generous Giving. "Stories." https://generousgiving.org/stories/?_radio_categories=legacy.

22. Ron Blue Institute. "Ron Blue Institute Latest Articles." https://ronblueinstitute.com/articles/.

23. RonaldBlueTrust. "Financial Services." https://www.ronblue.com/.

24. Akṣapāda. *Through the Eyes of Socrates: 420 Philosophical Aphorisms Unraveling Reality.*

25. Fontana, Francesca. "Covid-19 Forced Many Unprepared Young Adults to Deal with Their Parents' Estates." Wall Street Journal. May 1, 2021. https://www.wsj.com/articles/covid-19-parents-estates-11619815160.

26. Ritenbaugh, John W. "Ecclesiastes 7:11–12." The Berean Church of the Great God. https://www.theberean.org/index.cfm/main/default/id/9115/ver/amp/ecclesiastes-7-11-12.htm#:~:text=Daily%20Verse%20and%20Comment%20for%20Ecclesiastes%207%3A11-12%20Ecclesiastes,preserves%20the%20life%20of%20him%20who%20has%20it.

27. James. "It's Not How Much You Make, But How Much You Save." Simple Living Daily. April 10, 2018. https://simplelivingdaily.com/its-not-how-much-you-make-but-how-much-you-save/.

28. Alcorn, Randy. *The Treasure Principle: Unlocking the Secret of Joyful Giving.* Crown Publishing Group, 2017, p. 60.

29. Alcorn, *The Treasure Principle*, p. 100.

30. Eckman, Jim. "The State of the American Family in 2020." Issues in Perspective. September 19, 2020. http://issuesinperspective.com/2020/09/the-state-of-the-american-family-in-2020/.

31. Pew Research Center. "Religion and Living Arrangements Around the World." December 12, 2019. https://www.pewforum.org/2019/12/12/religion-and-living-arrangements-around-the-world/.

32. McLanahan, S., and G. Sandefur. *Growing Up with a Single Parent: What Hurts, What Helps.* Harvard University Press, 2009, p. 38.

33. Covey, Stephen. *The 7 Habits of Highly Effective Families.* St. Martin's Griffin, 1997.

34. Goldenwood. "What Dreams Do You Have?" https://goldenwoodnyc.org/dreamforum.

35. Greear, J. D. "Seven Ways to Overcome Satan." J. D. Greear Ministries. April 26, 2017. https://jdgreear.com/seven-ways-overcome-satan/.

36. Bradley, Jayson D. "Church Giving Statistics, 2019 Edition." Pushpay. July 18, 2018. https://pushpay.com/blog/church-giving-statistics/#:~:text=Tithers%20only%20make%20up%2010%E2%80%932 5%20percent%20of%20any,to%20the%20church%20is%20less%20than %20a%20quarter.

37. Pursue God. "A Heavenly Perspective: The Story of LeTourneau." https://www.pursuegod.org/a-heavenly-perspective-the-story-of-letourneau/.

38. Science of Generosity. "What Is Generosity?" University of Notre

Dame. https://generosityresearch.nd.edu/more-about-the-initiative/what-is-generosity/.

39. Generous Giving. https://generousgiving.org.

40. The National Christian Foundation. "Do You Have a Giving Strategy?" https://www.ncfgiving.com.

41. Ramsey, Dave. "The Quickest Right Way to Become a Millionaire." https://www.ramseysolutions.com.

42. Science of Generosity. "Learn More About Science of Generosity Initiative." University of Notre Dame. https://generosityresearch.nd.edu.

43. Ron Blue Institute. "Ron Blue Institute." https://ronblueinstitute.com.

44. Alcorn, *The Treasure Principle*, p. 100.

Made in the USA
Las Vegas, NV
29 November 2022